# Haitian Democracy Restored

## 1991 - 1995

Roland I. Perusse
Inter American Institute

University Press of America, Inc.
Lanham • New York • London

Copyright © 1995 by the
Inter American Institute

## University Press of America®, Inc.
4720 Boston Way
Lanham, Maryland 20706

3 Henrietta Street
London WC2E 8LU England

Copublished by arrangement with the
Inter American Institute.

**Library of Congress Cataloging-in-Publication Data**
Perusse, Roland I.
Haitian democracy restored, 1991-1995 / by Roland I. Perusse
p. cm.
Includes bibliographical references and index.
1. Haiti—Politics and government—1986- 2. Democracy—Haiti—
History. 3. United States—Relations—Haiti. 4. Haiti—Relations—
United States. I. Title.

F1928.2.P47   1995                          95-8761
320.97294'09'049—dc20                       CIP

ISBN 0-8191-9951-6 (cloth: alk paper)
ISBN 0-8191-9952-4 (pbk.: alk paper)

Printed in the United States of America

⊖™ The paper used in this publication meets the minimum
requirements of American National Standard for Information
Sciences—Permanence of Paper for Printed Library Materials,
ANSI Z39.48–1984.

# Dedication

To all the Haitian people who lost their lives in the military coup that took place in Haiti in 1991 and during the three heart-wrenching years that followed.

# Contents

# Preface

This book is a study of international conflict resolution of a complex cross-cultural crisis involving many actors: The Organization of American States, the United Nations and many individual nations and their respective bureaucracies and power structures. Thus it synthesizes a great deal of information from many sources over the period 1991 to 1995. Especially useful have been articles and commentary from *The Washington Post*, *The Washington Times* and *The New York Times*; newscasts and public affairs programs, mainly from ABC, CBS, CNN, NBC and PBS; attendance at or participation in panels and professional conferences on Haiti. Relevant documents were used from the United Nations, the Organization of American States, the White House, the U.S. Congress, the U.S. Department of State, the Washington Office on Haiti and various research organizations. Interviews were also conducted with and background briefings received from individuals working on Haitian affairs during this period.

It is my ardent hope that the lessons in conflict resolution which emerge from this sturdy will contribute in some small way to the prompt resolution, if not avoidance, of problems emanating from the overthrow of democratic governments by the military leaders of small Third World nations.

> Roland I. Perusse  
> Washington, D. C.  
> 1995

# Introduction

Some persons may challenge the title of this book. They would argue that democracy has never existed in Haiti and that it is a *non-sequitur* to speak about the restoration of something that has never existed. There is no question that democracy never existed in Haiti before December 20, 1990, but on that day the Reverend Jean-Bertrand Aristide, a Roman Catholic priest, was elected President of Haiti by two-thirds of the voters in an election certified as fair, free and honest by neutral international observers. It was held under a democratic constitution specifically designed to prevent the kind of dictatorships which had plagued Haiti in the past.

It is true that the democracy that functioned in Haiti during the brief tenure of Father Aristide was of short duration, that it was not the kind of democracy one finds in the United States and Western Europe or even in most parts of Latin America. Aristide, himself, was hardly a model democratic leader. But it was democracy nonetheless, especially when compared with the authoritarian rule which existed in Haiti during the previous 200 years of Haitian history and the three years after he was deposed.

We might ask ourselves, what constitutes democracy? Is there a yardstick by which one can judge whether democracy existed in Haiti under Aristide's first eight months in office, before his overthrow?

*The American Heritage Dictionary* is one of the most highly respected and authorative references for definitions and explanation of concepts. For the word democracy, we find the following entry in its Third Edition dated 1992:

1. Government of the people, exercised either directly or through their elected representatives.
2. A political or social unit which has such government.
3. The common people considered as the primary source of power.
4. Majority rule.
5. The principles of social equality and respect for the individual within a community.

Without question, the government of Aristide met the first four criteria. However, the last of these, social equality and respect for the individual has never existed throughout Haitian history. Aristide made an attempt to bridge the gap between rich and poor during his first eight months in office but made little progress. In fact his efforts at social reform were the principal reason for his ouster in the military coup of September 30, 1991.

The conclusion to be reached is that democracy under Aristide in 1991 was not perfect, but it was democracy nonetheless, and certainly democracy compared with the governments that preceded him and the government that succeeded him. He made a good start toward instituting democracy in Haiti, and his efforts should not be denigrated.

Perfection in democracy is an ideal rarely achieved in practice. Accusations of undemocratic behavior by Aristide are difficult to substantiate. What is clear is that he sought to fulfill the will of the people who elected him, and he showed deep respect for the constitution he was sworn to defend.

Obviously, President Clinton believed that democracy existed in Haiti under Aristide. His simplified explanation of U.S. policy toward Haiti during the crisis there, which he expressed over and over again during that period, was "to restore Aristide and democracy to Haiti."

It is often said or written that Jean-Bertrand Aristide was the first freely elected President in Haitian history. According to Ambassador Michael Barall, Deputy Chief of Mission of the U.S. Embassy in Haiti in the 1950s, Francois (Papa Doc) Duvalier was elected in a free election in 1957. But this is disputed by Robert Debs Heinl and Nancy Gordon Heinl in their well-researched book, *Written in Blood*, Houghton Mifflin, 1978.

*****

As of the beginning of 1995, restoration of democracy in Haiti was progressing well. Military authority was scheduled to transfer from the United States to the United Nations on March 31, 1995. Measures for international aid to Haiti were underway, and new parliamentary elections were tentatively planned for May 1995. They were expected to give the Aristide government greater legitimacy. Also, progress was being made on the difficult task of reforming the army, police and judicial system.

## Introduction

On January 29, 1995, the United Nations Security Council adopted a resolution declaring that the U.S.-led multinational intervention force had established a secure and stable environment in Haiti and set March 31, 1995 as the date for the transfer of peacekeeping duties from the United States to the United Nations Mission in Haiti. The mission would operate for 10 months until February 1996. It would consist of about 6,000 troops, 900 police officers, 227 civilian staff members, 193 local employees and 27 UN volunteers.

Its Commander would be U.S. Maj. Gen. Joseph W. Kinter, who would be technically under the authority of the United Nations Secretary General rather than the United States. Its rule of engagement would be to open fire only in self-defense. Its mandate would be to sustain a secure environment in Haiti and train a 1,500-member army and 4,000-member police force to take over responsibility for internal security when the mission would leave. It would also organize the elections planned for May 1995. The mission's budget would be $178 million for the first six months, with the United States paying one-third.

Although this shift of responsibility had been planned from the very beginning as Stage II of the UN-authorized intervention in Haiti, no specific date had been set or could have been anticipated. This early transition date was chosen in part because of strong pressure by the U.S. Congress for all American troops to leave Haiti. Though their numbers had been reduced from a peak of 21,000 to 7,100, and only one casualty had occurred, the operation was costly at a time Congress was trying to balance the national budget. In fact, Congress was threatening to cut off U.S. funds for all United Nations peacekeeping operations everywhere.

With only a fledgling government in operation, a surge in street crime and some anti-Aristide paramilitary groups still lurking in the countryside, disorganized but not destroyed, the work of the U.N. mission would not be easy.

On the economic front an international doners meeting in Paris approved a $660 million reconstruction program for Haiti and pledged $240 million in additional assistance. Long-awaited aid from the World Bank and International Monetary Fund was expected by mid-1995. The idea was launched to shift some U.S. textile quotas on apparel imports to Haiti, and the inefficient Electric Company of Haiti was scheduled for privatization.

The key to restoration of democracy in Haiti lies in civilian control of the army and police and in an impartial judicial system. All three institutions were undergoing drastic reforms early in 1995.

Aristide decided that henceforth the army would play a minor role in Haitian society and reduced the number of troops from 7,000 to 1,500 and replaced the military leadership with officers loyal to himself. There was some pressure to abolish the army altogether, but for some reason the United States insisted that Haiti needed some kind of non-political military force. Aristide accepted this advice but kept the institution weak to be sure it would never be able to carry out another coup. Symbolically, the military headquarters, a beautiful colonial building across the plaza from the National Palace, long a symbol of military power, was turned over to a newly-established Ministry of Women's Affairs.

The U.S. Agency for International Development agreed to provide $5 million to a program for retraining about 3,000 demobilized soldiers for civilian jobs, in part to prevent discontent from arising among them, but also to help overcome the shortage of technical specialists in Haitian society.

Aristide's promotion of Lt. Col. Pierre Cherubin to brigadier general, placing him next in line to be commander-in-chief, raised some eyebrows. Cherubin was believed by many to have been involved in the cover-up of a murder, apparently by the police, of five students in 1981. Two other officers more directly involved in the killings were working close to Aristide.

With the approximate reversal in numbers of personnel, the balance of power and responsibility for the maintenance of internal security in Haiti shifted from the army to the police. Indicative of the shift was the transformation of *Camp d'Aplication*, headquarters of the now-disbanded army Heavy Weapons Unit, into a new police academy for the preparation of a new permanent police force.

Its first class of 375 officers had begun their training and were expected to graduate in June 1995. The underlining theme of the instruction was respect for human rights, human dignity, repect for law, community policing and basic police procedures. Veteran police officers from Canada, France, Norway and the United States served on the faculty. The first women were admitted to the police force, and an internal affairs office was set up to monitor abuses. The basic aim was to have an efficient police force in place by the time the United Nations Mission in Haiti was scheduled to leave in February 1996.

The U.S. Department of Justice International Criminal Investigative Training Assistance Program was committed to investing $50 million in the police reorientation program over the next five years.

At least as important as building an efficient police force is creating a fair and impartial penal and judicial system. Otherwise the police would have little incentive to do their job. If Aristide's policy of "reconciliation, not revenge," was to succeed, the populace had to be reassured that those who violated the civil rights of others received punishment to fit their crimes; otherwise "street justice" would replace court justice.

UN Secretary General Boutrous Boutrous-Ghali wrote in a report, "Judicial officials are inadequate in number and quality, and their lack of support outstanding . . . . In a few places judicial officials of some competence command a degree of public confidence. But in many more areas, the situation is confused, and the system is not functioning."

He could have added, but he was probably too much of a diplomat to do so, that corruption in the system was rampant, that there was a three-year backlog in criminal cases, that the prisons were overloaded with people waiting for their cases to be heard, and that many of the most notorious human rights offenders remained free or had gone underground.

Parliament authorized establishment of a Commission on Justice and Truth, modeled on a UN-mandated panel in El Salvador to investigate past human rights violations there. Aristide appointed a prominent sociologist, Francois Bauchard, to head the commission, but no office had yet been set up.

With the resignation of Minister of Justice Ernst Mallebranche, who had strongly resisted changes in the department, hope appeared for reform. The government undertook what it termed a "recycling program" for judges and prosecuters. Several hundred were expected to take a five-day course to be conducted by the Office of Professional Development and Training and the National Center for State Courts, both part of the U.S. Department of Justice.

All in all, democracy was on its way to restoration in Haiti, but it still had a long way to go to become rooted and effective. A sound educational system needed to be established at all levels, and a literacy campaign undertaken. Vast improvements were required in health and nutrition. The bare hills had to be restored, through reforestration, to their natural beauty. Tolerance for opposing views and respect for one's fellowman had to be developed.

As far as the United States is concerned, the Haitian experience also sends us messages. There is a strong need to review U.S. immigration policy so as to apply it uniformly and avoid discrimination. The Department of State needs to develop better expertise on developing nations. The Central Intelligence Agency must be kept in close rein on intelligence operations in countries like Haiti.

There needs to be greater concern in our goverrment on human rights abuses in Third World countries. Our nation needs more men like Captain Lawrence P. Rockwood, counter intelligence officer of the U.S. Army 10th Mountain Division, who took President Clinton at his word when he said protection of human rights in Haiti was in the U.S. national interest and risked courtmartial for investigating and reporting on the inhumane conditions at the Port-au-Prince National Penetentiary. And there needs to be better coordination of policy within the U.S. Government to avoid mixed signals and conflicting views to the outside world. We must also give more rather than less attention to the practice of multilateral diplomacy.

\*\*\*\*\*

Some persons have asked what stimulated me to write this book. My answer is simple: it had to be written by someone. The coup against Aristide was unjust, illegal and immoral. The suffering which ensued within Haiti and on the high seas was too much for the world to ignore. By reporting on the dimensions of this tragedy, on how senseless it was, perhaps it would never be repeated. By studying how the international community coped with these problems, we can take note of both the errors made and the strategies that worked in case, God forbid, another crisis on this pattern should arise again in the future.

In closing, I want to thank my good friend and colleague, Dr. Anne Greene, author of the recent book, *The Catholic Church in Haiti: Political and Social Change*, for her kindness in reviewing the manuscript for this book and making numerous suggestions that helped improve it; also my patient and understanding wife, Luz Amalia Perusse, who typed the manuscript for publication and in the process caught many errors I inadvertently made in the original draft.

# Chapter I

# Aristide the Man

Jean-Bertrand Aristide, the parish priest turned president, is certainly one of the most controversial personalities on the world scene today. Evaluations of this man vary from adulation and worship by his followers to charges of murderer and psychopath by his enemies and detractors. Sentiment is polarized between these two extremes. An objective appraisal of his life and work lies somewhere in between. The challenge of this chapter is to arrive at such an objective appraisal based on an evaluation of his character and life experience, using available data from many sources, much of it conflicting and contradictory.

In terms of physical appearance, Aristide does not make much of an impression. He is small, frail looking, some five feet tall, weighing about 130 pounds. He wears large, gold-rimmed glasses and looks like a scholar (which he is), rather than a priest or politician. He is quiet and soft-spoken in general conversation but dramatic, persuasive and illuminating in public oratory, especially when he speaks in his native Creole, which he laces with allegorical proverbs.

## *The Early Years*

Jean-Bertrand Aristide had humble beginnings. He was born on July 15, 1953 in Port Salut, a small village near Les Cayes, in the southwest portion of the island, in a small house in the hills, barren of trees, in an area without roads, water, electricity or much agriculture. The family were peasants, but owned their own land. His father died shortly after his birth. Aristide was greatly influenced by his grandfather who was strongly imbued by the work ethic and, as an informal rural leader, practiced a rural brand of constructive social justice.

Young Aristide and his mother and sister spent their winters in Port-au-Prince where they joined others of the extended family, along with friends and neighbors. In his autobiography, Aristide calls this a "communitarian existence," a "socialist reality on a small scale." In the summer he would return to Port Salut, where he states in his autobiography "cooperation and egalitarian social organization" were essential to furnish food for each family.

Finally, Aristide and his mother and sister settled permanently in Port-au-Prince where he started school at the age of five with the Catholic order, the Salesian Brothers. He, as well as the other students in his class, were forced to learn French and were punished if they spoke Creole. At the time Aristide accepted this punishment as part of the learning process. Only later in life did he sense injustice in this type of academic methodology.

Aristide excelled in school. Nonetheless, he received corporal punishment if he did not live up to the high demands placed upon him by his teachers. He learned French, Latin and Greek and began to study English, Spanish and Italian. He remained at this school until he was fourteen, then entered the Notre Dame secondary school in preparation for the priesthood. His educational formation was directed toward service to the poor. At eighteen, he says, he felt himself a citizen of the world.

After graduating from the seminary at the age of 21, Aristide spent a novice year in the Dominican Republic. On his return to Port-au-Prince, he attended the National University of Haiti, graduating in 1979 with a degree in psychology. As a radio commentator and preacher, he became an active militant against the traditional church, insisting that the Vatican should give priority to the poor. As a result, he was "persuaded" by his superiors to travel to Israel for biblical studies. There he added Hebrew and Arabic to his repertoire of languages. He returned to Haiti in 1982, was ordained to the priesthood and appointed to the parish of St. Joseph in Port-au-Prince. He served there only three months. An "error" in his appointment was noted by the dictatorial Duvalier regime and he was sent to Canada for "pastoral reorientation." He continued his graduate studies at the University of Montreal, completing a master's degree in biblical theology as well as course work for a doctorate in psychology.

In 1985 he returned to Haiti via another exile study detour, this time to Greece. From 1979 to 1985, a period of six years, he spent only a few months in his native Haiti and nearly six years in exile.

Aristide speaks four languages fluently: French, English, Spanish and his native Creole. His Creole is sharp and biting and occasionally difficult to decipher because he tends to speak in allegorical metaphors. He is self-taught in Italian and Hebrew and has a working knowledge of Latin.

As a result of his many "exiles" by the Salasian order, he has lived in the Dominican Republic, Italy, Israel, Canada and Greece. Following the 1991 coup which drove him from office, he took refuge in Venezuela and the United States.

## *Aristide as Parish Priest*

We have mentioned Aristide's first assignment as parish priest which lasted only three months before being aborted by the Duvalier regime. His second assignment, on his return to Haiti in 1985, was to teach biblical theology in the major seminary in Port-au-Prince and at the same time to serve as master of studies at the National School for Arts and Crafts in the parish of St. Jean Bosco.

In his autobiography, Aristide tells us that he had no intention of limiting himself to this kind of teaching. The struggle to uproot President Jean-Claude Duvalier had entered a decisive phase. He leaped into the fray, mobilizing thousands of young people to demonstrations. During a service at the church of St. Jean Bosco, he escaped the first of what would be a long series of attempts to kill him. A *Tonton Macoute* who had come to assassinate him was disarmed by members of the congregation at the last moment. The man was about to draw his revolver during the celebration of the eucharist. His gun was taken away from him, and he was beaten by young members of the church. The man had been paid to shoot Aristide. If he had carried out his mission, a passport and visa for leaving the country were ready for him.

By the end of 1985 St. Jean Bosco had emerged as one of the principal centers of resistance to *Macoute* rule. It was subject to repeated violent attacks and massacres. On the last of these, its church was burned to the ground. His followers organized themselves as *Ti legliz,* "the little ones of the church," and adopted the slogan, "This is only a beginning; let us continue to fight."

On May 16, 1986, the Salesians ordered Aristide to desist from further participation in politics. For a time he obeyed, but in November participated in a march of two hundred thousand in protest of arbitrary government.

Aristide said "I had the feeling that I was acting as a theologian in order to give direction to the political struggle." In a more orthodox role for a priest, he organized a center for homeless children that he christened "The Family Selavi."

The Council of National Government demanded that Aristide be banished, and the *Macoutes* that he be eliminated. In August 1987 a superior came from Rome. The Vatican had condemned liberation theology and Aristide was given three days to prepare for his transfer to Croix-des-Maisons, about six miles from Port-au-Prince. But the young people prevented him from leaving, and the Salesians were forced to relent.

In 1988, two weeks before Christmas, Aristide was expelled from the Salesian order. The decree for his dismissal stated:

> His attitude has had a negative effect on his confrères . . . his selfishness demonstrates a lack of sincerity and religious and priestly consciousness.

The judgment cited

> the impossibility of a sincere and fruitful dialogue . . . incitement to hatred and violence, and a glorifying of the class struggle, . . . the profanation of the liturgy. . . . Father Jean-Bertrand Aristide has always preferred to distance himself from the concrete demands of the community, becoming a protagonist of the destabilization of the community of the faithful; and he has done so in a constant, public and incisive manner, so that the organs of the press and groups of varied origins present him as the "leader of the popular church" in Haiti.

In his autobiography Aristide stated defiantly: "Let there be no doubt: my expulsion from the Salesians has not changed my Christian conscience, blunted my fidelity to the dispossessed, nor cooled the burning questions I addressed to the Catholic heirarchy."

# *Personality*

Aristide is charismatic and candid, with caustic humor. He can mesmerize an audience with his oratory. He is a modern Don Quixote, attacking evil where he sees it — in the Haitian military, the *Tonton Macoutes* and what he interprets as U.S. imperialism. By his own admission, he is a "refusenik," a rebel. By nature, he is frank and outspoken, sometimes inappropriately. For example, at his inauguration, a day for celebration, he announced that all generals, except one whose loyalty he admired, were to be retired, "to remove any cause for discord between the army and the people." He is uncompromising and stubborn in his struggle against dictatorship and oppression. On the other hand, he is a fair and sensitive person. In his few months in office, he did much to close the gap in earnings between the rich and the poor. As president, he included himself in his salary reforms, assigning himself a salary of only $4,000 a month, the same as that of his cabinet ministers. He has always lived modestly, as a student, a priest and as president. During his exile in the United States following the coup that displaced him from office, he moved from a luxury apartment in the fashionable section of Georgetown, Washington, D.C. to simple quarters near the Chinese section of the city, to avoid accusations of ostentation or reckless expenditure.

One can not question his courage and unselfishess. At one point in his tenure as parish priest, he entered the notorious Fort Dimanche prison at 10 p.m. and talked his way into the release of a group of his followers who had been arrested that morning for participation in a symbolic funeral for that den of torture, starvation and disappearances. He, himself, might have been taken prisoner, but, as a result of an hour of polite patter and flattery, he was able to induce the chief of the prison to release the captives to his custody.

As U.S. negotiators learned, Aristide is a man of principle. Some called him stubborn and obstinate when he resisted all attempts to return him to Haiti as a figurehead, to compromise unduly with his opponents, to form a coalition government with the opposition, when he had received 67% of the vote. One might ask, would it have been proper for President Clinton, who received little more than one third of the popular vote in the 1992 U.S. presidential election, to have been asked by outsiders to incorporate George Bush and Ross Perot into his cabinet?

By his own admission, Aristide succumbs briefly to bouts of depression, but to call him a manic depressive, as has been done by some of his critics, is a gross exaggeration. His reactions to brutality, repression and dictatorship are visceral, only later rational and analytical. He is not a grand strategist nor a plotter, and he is not much of a team player, though he is capable of cooperation in critical situations. He believes in inspiration and is confident that his insights will lead him in the right direction, and they usually do. He has an overriding concern for the needy and the poor.

## *Basic Beliefs and Convictions*

Below is a list of some of the more basic beliefs and convictions of President Aristide. They are based mainly on his own expressed views and actions as cited in his books *Jean-Bertrand Aristide: An Autobiography* and *In the Parish of the Poor*. These are referenced as AB and PP in the citations which follow.

## *Political Beliefs and Convictions*

1. Aristide's preaching was based on liberation theology, the freeing of the masses from their inferior position in society.
2. Though he admits having been accused of being a bad Catholic priest and a demagogic politician and one who praises communism, he claims that marxism is not one of his sources of inspiration (p.68, AB).
3. He claims that his political strategy is non-violence and collective resistance.
4. He has immense respect for the Haitian constitution and the constitutional process. He was asked many times if he would publicly support an invasion of Haiti to restore him to his position as Chief of State in Haiti. He has steadfastly refused to do so, claiming that this would lead to his impeachment. In his oath of office, imbedded in the Haitian constitution (Article 135-1), he is sworn to maintain the nation's independence and the integrity of its territory.
5. Aristide frequently expressed anti-U.S. views during his years in opposition in Haiti. For example, in a radio message September 11, 1988, he claimed that

The U.S. Government, along with its lackeys among the Haitian elite, has already begun to conspire to infiltrate *Macoutes* into the Army, to buy off soldiers, to sow corruption, to plant divisions, and to multiply spies. (p. 97, PP)

6. He has called the United States a military dictatorship and claims that the United States has exploited Haiti. (pp. 7, 11 PP)
7. Aristide considered Che Guevara, a Cuban rebel leader who operated in Latin America, to be close to his own values. (p. 126 AB)
8. Aristide has preached revolution and class warfare:

   One day the people under that table (the table of the rich) will rise up in righteousness and knock the table of privilege over, and take what rightfully belongs to them. (p. 9, PP)

9. One of Aristide's rallying cries, which struck fear in the elite, was *rache mamyok,* a Creole expression meaning to uproot manioc from a field. It was aimed at removing Duvalierists and militarist elements from the country.
10. Aristide has termed capitalism "a deadly economic infection" and "a mortal sin" (pp. 6-7, PP) and has called on Haiti to make "an historic turn to the left."

## *Social Beliefs and Convictions*

1. Aristide claims that he does not judge a person by the faith that person professes but by his or her behavior.
2. Aristide does not consider voodoo to be antagonistic to the Christian faith. The true *hougan* (voodoo priest), he claims, gives reality to the community's faith.
3. Aristide has fought for the equality of women.
4. Aristide believes that the main mission of the church should be to improve the lot of the poor.
5. He believes in the power of love and truth to turn back violence, hatred, falsehood and injustice (p. 108, AB).
6. He believes that human liberation does not necessarily occur through violence. It is possible, he says, to struggle for justice and peace without killing people. (p. 109, AB).
7. Aristide is convinced of the hypocricy of the church of Rome (p. 21, PP).
8. Aristide believes it is the obligation of large land owners to give land to the poor.

In an interview in New York in October 1993, Aristide sought to show that his long exile in Washington had made him a more measured politician. When he returns to Haiti, he said, "I will have to listen to the prime minister and the government, to be close to them, to build justice and reconciliation." In radio broadcasts to the people of Haiti in 1994, he promised such reconcilation.

Aristide spoke about making "a new beginning for building a state of law." He said it had been a "privilege" to forge new ties with the private sector, through overtures organized by Prime Minister Robert Malval, an Aristide appointee and one of the few wealthy businessmen to support him in his 1990 campaign.

In a speech to the UN General Assembly on September 30, 1993, two years after his deposition from office in Haiti, Aristide called upon all Haitians to put aside vengeance.

In a speech on July 1994 he outlined a 10-point plan of military, judicial and tax reform, and a plan for universal health care and education for his impoverished nation. He also promised to promote the goals of the private sector, the capitalists he had previously condemned.

## Accusations by his Detractors

At some time or other, Aristide has been accused of being a demagogue, a communist, a mixture of Robin Hood, Robespierre and Che Guevara, and much more. But the most serious accusations against him are related to his mental health and his record on human rights. The principal vehicle for their dissemination has been a "psychological profile" which is classified Secret, and was issued by the Central Intelligence Agency of the Government of the United States in 1991, and reissued in 1993.

The CIA Profile, which has never been made public, deals mainly with Aristide's presumed psychological problems, such as bouts of depression and his "being out of touch with reality." The *Profile* claims that in 1990 he was treated by psychiatrists in two hospitals in Montreal, Canada for megalomia and manic-depressive illness. After being briefed on this report, U.S. Senator Jesse Helms of North Carolina branded Aristide a psychopath. President Clinton, Vice President Gore and others in the Clinton administration certified that they found Aristide reasonable to deal with, but this did not stop the accusations. They were difficult to refute because their security classifications prevented precise knowledge of their content except to a privileged few.

Finally, this CIA accusation was discredited by some brilliant investigative reporting by Christopher Marquis, a staff writer for the *Miami Herald.*

Marquis obtained the name of the hospital at which the CIA reported Aristide had been treated and persuaded Aristide to write him a letter authorizing him to request from this and three other Montreal hospitals all records relating to any psychiatric treatment he may have received. All four hospitals certified they had no record of ever having treated Aristide. Obviously, no one at the CIA had ever checked the veracity of the accusation.

Professor Melvin Goodman at the National War College in Washington, D.C., himself a former CIA agent, claimed that the CIA's assessment of Aristide was distorted because of its ties with the Haitian military.

On November 1, 1993, *The New York Times* reported that key members of the military regime then controlling Haiti had been paid by the CIA for information from the mid-1980s at least until the 1991 coup which forced Aristide from power. The article also stated that, in a 1992 report circulated in Washington, Brian Latell, the CIA analyst who briefed Congress on the Aristide *Profile*, once praised Lt. Col. Raoul Cédras, Haiti's military dictator, as one of "the most promising group of Haitian leaders to emerge since the Duvalier dictatorship was removed in 1986."

The *Miami Herald* editorialized that "the CIA has a long and unsavory history of letting its political bias taint its analysis."

Whatever the motivation for the second edition of the *Profile*, its timing was disastrous from the standpoint of U.S. policy toward Haiti. It was nothing less than character assassination, and it came at a moment the White House was contemplating the use of force to return Aristide to Haiti, as called for by the Governors Island Agreement. In view of the *Profile*, it was highly unlikely that the U.S. Congress would have approved any U.S. military action on behalf of Aristide at that time. The CIA *Profile* had accomplished its purpose.

In the area of human rights, the principal charge against Aristide is that he advocated "necklacing," which is a criminal practice that originated in South Africa and involves placing a tire over the neck of a victim and setting it on fire. In a speech given in Port-au-Prince on September 27, 1991, three days before his overthrow, Aristide expressed a hope that "in accordance with the Constitution, we will build together a strong opposition on the basis of the law." He repeatedly urged the crowd that if they catch an embezzler or *Tonton Macoute*, "Do not fail to give him what he deserves." However, each of these exhortations was linked to the Constitution. In particular, Aristide referred to Article 291 of the Constitution which excludes *Macoutes* from public office.

The speech, as translated from the Creole by the CIA's own Foreign Broadcast Information Service, employs metaphor, humor, and colorful rhetoric, so its message is not always clear. On its face, however, the speech seems to be a call for using constitutional means to fight representatives of the former Haitian regime.

The reference most quoted, to "necklacing" as being a "beautiful tool" that "smells good;" "wherever you go, you feel like smelling it" follows an extended series of metaphors that compares the Constitution of Haiti to a tool, an instrument, a device, a trowel and a bugle ("Your tool is in your hands. Your instrument is in your hands. Your Constitution is in your hands.") Immediately after the passage about the "good smell" comes the observation, "It is provided for by the Constitution, which bans *Macoutes* from political activity."

Aristide made no specific mention of "necklacing" or violence anywhere in his speech, but Aristide's critics and some independent observers have accused him of intending a hidden meaning, perhaps a warning, that if constitutional means are not effective against opponents of democracy, then violence may be necessary.

As a matter of fact the human rights record of Aristide's eight-month administration is good, especially as compared with that of his predecesors. According to human rights groups, there were seven political lynchings during Aristide's brief time in office, and there is no evidence that they were approved or condoned by Aristide. The victims were usually soldiers or Duvalierists who had been accused of murder. In contrast, there were at least 50 political lynchings in the 11 months before Aristide took office.

It is impossible to arrive at a definitive number of civilians killed by the military and its allies since the coup which overthrew Aristide. However, 5,000 is believed to be a conservative estimate. Though the human rights record of Aristide while in office is not perfect, it represents a great improvement over previous years and is vastly superior to the ever-mounting toll of the illegal military regime that followed.

In conclusion, Aristide is neither a god nor a psychopath nor a murderer. He is a highly intelligent human being who has shown great concern for the well-being of his people, especially the poor, the underprivileged and the down-trodden.

At the height of attacks against Aristide in 1993, Bishop Thomas Gumble of Detroit released a letter signed by 27 U.S. Catholic bishops which stated that "President Aristide has been a model of true leadership, and among modern heads of state he stands out for his consistent and courageous calls for non-violent change."

The bottom line is this: Aristide was elected by 67% of the voters of Haiti in an election certified by international observers as free and fair. Who are we to question the wisdom and judgment of the people of Haiti? Few human beings are perfect. If and when Aristide should choose to run again for public office, the people of Haiti will have another chance to accept or reject him. In the meantime, he deserves our support as he fills out the remainder of his term in Haiti.

# Chapter II

# Aristide's First Eight Months

It is a common error to refer to the length of Aristide's tenure as President of Haiti, in Haiti in 1991 as being of seven months duration. Actually, eight months would be closer to the facts. He was inaugurated on February 7, 1991 and deposed by a coup on September 30, 1991, six days short of eight calendar months. Hence, it is more accurate to round out the time frame to eight months. How the erroneous citation of seven months originated, and why it has been repeated so often by so many is difficult to fathom. Perhaps it is another illustration of the lemming phenomenon.

Be that as it may, this chapter will cover the major developments in Haiti during the turbulent period, January 1 to September 30, 1991, concentrating in particular on Aristide's inauguration, his reforms and accomplishments, growing discontent on the part of those sectors of society adversely affected, and the resultant military coup of September 30.

In 1990, demonstrations brought down a military government and new elections were scheduled for December 16. At first, Aristide resisted all calls to become a candidate, saying he preferred to remain a disinterested spokesman. But the masses of his supporters pressed him to compete. He finally gave in to their pleas and registered on the last possible day. Though his campaign was brief, his views were well known, and he won 67% of the vote in an election deemed fair and honest by all disinterested observers. The next closest candidate to Aristide, Marc Bazin, an international banker with connections to the United States, received only 14% of the vote. Aristide's party also gained control of both houses of the legislature.

Aristide attributed his victory to a movement he called *lavalas*, a Creole word for the torrent of water that rushes down Haiti's denuded hillsides after a rainstorm, sweeping debris before it and having a purifying effect.

## The Inauguration

The principle of the *lavalas* was applied to the city of Port-au-Prince, as followers of Aristide celebrated by arming themselves with shovels, rakes, brooms and brushes, swept the streets of debris and decorated the city with red and white paint.

But the number of high-ranking world leaders in attendance was disappointing. The war in the Persian Gulf had just begun and the principal chiefs of state and heads of government with interests in Haiti found themselves involved in critical military operations. Nevertheless, the United States was represented by former president Jimmy Carter, and France by Madame Danielle Mitterand, in representation of her husband. Also present was Carlos Andrés Pérez, president of Venezuela, and dignitaries from most of the Caribbean countries.

The act of inauguration took place in the national palace, the gleaming white edifice in the center of the Champs de Mars, and the highlight was the speech of the newly-elected President.

His most stunning announcement was that all the general officers except Hérard Abraham, whom Aristide considered most loyal to him, would be removed. It was a bold step, made at the zenith of his popularity, but it shocked the officer corps and solidified their opposition to the new regime.

Otherwise, the main theme of his discourse was an appeal for justice and solidarity. His concern for the welfare of the poor was reflected in promises of food and education for all. He was at the pinnacle of power, and his words inspired confidence in the future. But the question on everyone's mind was, Will he able to execute his promises for a better Haiti?

## Reforms and Accomplishments

In assessing the reforms of Aristide during his first eight months in office, it helps to remember that eight months is a short time for anyone to be in charge of a country with so many basic needs. No miracles should have been expected of him.

But Aristide made a good start. He trimmed the excesses and perks of the bureaucracy. His predecessor as president, Ertha Pascal Troiullot, enjoyed a salary $10,000 a year, supplemented by $15,000 for monthly expenses. He established his own salary, and the salary of his cabinet ministers at $4,000 a year. For the common worker he established a minimum wage of five dollars a day in major industries. He began to reform the judicial system and laid out plans for universal health care and for education for the poor.

In addition, Aristide instituted a war against corruption and smuggling that increased public revenues and avoided new taxes. He also laid plans for the establishment of cooperatives and to decentralize the economy to the countryside.

He was concerned about overpopulation in relation to resources. But he made clear that he had no intention of requiring anyone to practice contraception. Such a requirement, he said, would, more than any other, "violate the sphere of the most elementary freedoms."

Under Aristide Haiti was becoming a more secure, a more open, and a more productive society. The people were regaining their dignity and their liberty. Political and press freedom was established. The people felt more secure in their daily lives. The notorious Fort Dimanche prison was closed, the brutal section chiefs who controlled rural areas were disbanded, and the military was being changed to a professional corps. Human rights violations fell 75% during these nine months, and none of those that occurred were attributable to Aristide. And the World Bank showed a willingness to assist the new government. A new nation was about to be born!

## Discontent Rises

As often happens in life, doing what is necessary can lead to problems. As might be expected those persons adversely affected by Aristide's reforms were those most disturbed by his policies and actions. His war on drugs threatened the income of those who relied on this illegal trade as a source of wealth — principally the army and the police. His war on corruption disturbed those profiting from this evil practice, again the military and the police. Civil service reforms generated enemies in the bureaucracy among those benefitting from the existing system, which allowed them generous outside income and inside privileges.

The wealthy felt threatened by Aristide's policies. As previously indicated in Chapter II, he preached revolution and class warfare. In his speech of September 21, 1991, nine days before his overthrow, he warned the bourgeosie to share their wealth with the poor or face their wrath.

"You have only one choice," he told them. "Otherwise it is not going to be good for you. I have given you seven months to straighten out, and the seven months have ended today." Some businessmen actually helped finance the coup.

But it was among the military that Aristide encountered most resistance. His efforts to reform the army resulted in accusations of interference in military affairs. The dismissal of most of the high command and their replacement by junior officers more closely inclined toward democratic reform caused particular resentment. Above all, his creation of a 50-man presidential guard, trained by the Swiss, frightened the military, especially non-commissioned officers, who accused him of trying to set up his own private army.

## *The Coup of September 30, 1991*

For the military caste and the privileged, the recovery of spirit among the common people and fear of changes which might affect them adversely, were just too much.

On September 25, 1991, Aristide made a speech to the United Nations General Assembly in New York announcing that democracy was fully rooted in Haiti. He spoke on the theme of the "Ten Commandments of Democracy" as applied to Haiti:

1. Liberty or death
2. Democracy or death
3. Fidelity to human rights
4. The right to eat and work
5. The right to demand what rightfully belongs to us
6. Legitimate defense of the diaspora
7. No to violence, yes to *Lavalas*
8. Fidelity to the human being
9. Fidelity to our culture, and
10. Everyone around the same table

When Aristide returned to Haiti, there were already rumors of a coup. There was no question that his reforms and the pro-democracy speech had caused uneasiness, resentment and fright among the military and the privileged elite. On September 27, 1991 Aristide compounded their fears with a virulent speech to his followers in which he called for action to defend their newly-constituted democratic government.

Two mutinees caused some concern — one by soldiers in Petionville, the other by sailors in the navy — but Aristide attended to them personally and seemed to have defused both incidents.

In his autobiography, Aristide gives the following account of the coup:

> On the evening of Sunday, September 29, shots were heard at the Frères camp, a few kilometers from Port-au-Prince. This time the rumor of mutiny was transformed into the noise of automatic weapons. The director of the national radio, Michel Favard, a brave man, also announced that a coup d'état was imminent. He would be kidnapped immediately afterward by a military commando troop. Before they were cut off, the radio stations had called for vigilance against the suspicious movements of part of the army.
>
> On the previous evening, I had called General Cédras to ask his feeling about the rumors, to which I still gave little credence. He supported me in my skepticism, and we laughed about it together. How can I help feeling some remorse now, when I think of the thousands of dead and remember the tranquil calm I then felt, which at that time seemed to be so completely justified?
>
> Cédras, whom I had appointed head of the general staff on February 7, 1991, and later commander-in-chief of the army, had taken part in the organization of the elections in December 1990. He was a young officer of the new generation, commissioned in 1971, from a class born under Jean-Claude Duvalier. I had chosen to cultivate a good deal of confidence in our relationship. There was very little suspicion: he had often remarked on his attachment to the democratic process.
>
> On Sunday I received the same reassuring response from Cédras, but by evening there could be no more doubt about the rebellion: my house was surrounded and bullets were spattering against its walls again. Friends and militants who were already there or who came in great numbers were massacred. Before the demonstrators could assemble or barricades be erected, the military emptied their magazines at everything that moved. They had learned the lesson of Lafontant's coup d'état: at all costs, they had to prevent the people from gathering, barricades from being erected, and a popular insurrection from being unleashed. Assisted by *Macoute* bands apparently coming from the Dominican Republic, they sowed death everywhere. The corpses were counted in the tens and hundreds. The terror was carried out in the

brutal form in order to discourage any popular reaction. *Lafanmi Selavi* was a target once again, along with the populous neighborhoods (Cité-Soleil, Carrefour), where the people attempted with the most pitiful means to provide some opposition to the soldiery. The young partisans of *Lavalas* paid a heavy price.

The night was shattered by cries and by the incessant noise of automatic weapons. It was impossible for me to leave my house, which had been transformed into a bunker. It was equally impossible for me to send out an appeal that would be heard. The radio transmitters had been occupied or destroyed by the military, and the airwaves were hopelessly mute. I owe the fact that I emerged alive from my house to a few diplomats, especially the French ambassador, Jean-Raphael Dufour, who took the risk of coming to get me. A convoy was moving toward the presidential palace. One of our soldiers was killed. Along the route, we were attacked several times.

Had the whole army risen, or was this a mutiny by a few isolated units, supported by the *Macoute* leaders like *Franck Romain* or *William Régala*? As soon as we reached the National Palace, I called Cédras to get to the bottom of things.

It is a trick! The building is surrounded! I have only a few reliable friends with me. I try to leave with the others, to avoid a civil war. My object is to talk with them, to negotiate, perhaps to persuade them. Guns are crackling outside. One of those beside me falls dead. I have already experienced similar situations: I throw myself to the ground. Death is prowling closer. I have just obtained a new respite: but for how long?

One of our heroes, Captain Fritz Pierre-Louis, has been killed in cold blood. It is incredible but true; a crime, a horror. At the same time I feel, I know that my friends, my brothers and sisters who live crowded together in the lower city are under fire. We leave the palace as prisoners, headed for the army general headquarters. Cédras is there; he hid his cards very well. Smart and sprightly in the uniform of his high rank, he is smiling, calm, even cheerful and condescending. He tells me plainly, with a glowing countenance; "From now on, I am the president." Eight of my companions are tortured and beaten by the soldiers.

Cédras is pleased with himself. The officers drink to his health. There is the atmosphere of a macabre festival alongside the bloodied faces of my friends. I myself have my hands tied. They try to humiliate me. The military discuss my fate in loud tones. "We ought to kill him."

They almost get into an argument about who will have the pleasure of doing it. International reaction — France? the United States? — is worrisome to the more "political" among them. They hesitate. They deliberate, haggling over lives, mine in particular. The pressure applied by the democratic countries wins the day: I will leave, finally, on the plane sent by Carlos Andrés Pérez, the president of Venezuela, a friend whose tenacity is irresistible. (from *Aristide: An Autobiography*, Jean-Bertrand Aristide, Orbis Books, 1993)

Aristide had no way of knowing it at the time, but the coup against him was actually led by then Major Michel Francois of the Haitian police and a group of enlisted men. Francois sent a group of armed men to Cédras' home. Cédras was taken at gunpoint to military command headquarters, where Francois was waiting for him. Francois told Cédras to assume his role as general, or he would be killed or sent away. Cédras complied.

## Evaluation of First Eight Months

One of Aristide's basic problems is that the Haitian Constitution provides for a parliamentary rather than a presidential form of government. As president he sought to make executive decisions on his own with little or no consultation with the Haitian Senate and House of Delegates. The Prime Minister, though selected by the President, must be approved by the legislature and is considered a major political actor. The 1987 Constitution was written with an eye to putting an end to "president for life" dictatorships which have typified Haitian history. Aristide's failure to consult with the parliament on his reform measures resulted in considerable resentment within a body in which his party had numerical control.

During Aristide's brief tenure, democracy made tremendous strides. Not so much his policies as his tactics led to his downfall; also the speed at which he sought to execute change.

After the coup, Cédras and Francois rewarded themselves with promotions in rank — Cédras a double promotion from Brigadier General to Lieutenant General, Francois a single promotion from Major to Lieutenant Colonel.

# Chapter III

# Early Attempts at Restoration

Fortunately for Jean-Bertrand Aristide, the groundwork for his restoration as the legitimately-elected president of Haiti had already been laid out four months before the coup which deposed him. At the historic meeting of the General Assembly of the Organization of American States at Santiago, Chile, on June 5, 1991, the 34 active members of the Organization, all of them democracies, signed the famous Resolution 1080, commonly known as the Santiago Agreement. In its first operative paragraph the member states resolved:

> To instruct the Secretary General for the immediate convocation of a meeting of the Permanent Council in the event of any occurrences giving rise to the sudden or irregular interruption of the democratic political institutional process or of the legitimate exercise of power by the democratically elected government in any of the Organization's member states, in order, within the framework of the Charter, to examine the situation, decide on and convene an ad hoc meeting of the Ministers of Foreign Affairs, or a special session of the General Assembly, all of which must take place within a ten-day period.

When OAS Secretary General Joao Baena Soares learned during the morning of September 30, 1991 about the events occurring in Haiti, he immediately convoked a meeting of the Permanent Council of the Organization in Washington, D.C. The Honorable Jean Casimir, Haiti's ambassador to Washington and a Council member, reported that rebels in Haiti had captured the National Palace and that President Aristide was a prisoner at the general headquarters of the armed forces.

He reviewed the rebels' demands: their own general staff; the return to duty of military personnel thrown out of the army by former President Avril; the exile of military personnel returned to duty by President Aristide; retirement of Aristide's personal guard; total independence for the Police and the Army; police responsibility to the Ministry of Justice; and a halt to elimination from government of followers of the Duvaliers.

These, Casimir said, were unconstitutional demands that Aristide could not fulfill. He asked for the implementation of Resolution 1080, specifically to consider sending international observers to Haiti as soon as possible to monitor the observance or non-observance of human rights.

The Council unanimously condemned the coup and approved the following resolution:

CP/RES. 567 (870/91)
SUPPORT TO THE DEMOCRATIC GOVERNMENT OF HAITI
THE PERMANENT COUNCIL OF THE ORGANIZATION OF AMERICAN STATES,
BEARING IN MIND that representative democracy is the form of government of the region and that its effective exercise, consolidation, and enhancement are shared priorities;
REAFFIRMING that the principles enshrined in the OAS Charter and the ideals of peace, democracy, social justice, comprehensive development, and solidarity constitute permanent underpinnings of the inter-American system;
TAKING INTO ACCOUNT the grave events that have taken place in Haiti and that represent an abrupt, violent, and irregular interruption of the legitimate exercise of power by the democratic government of that country; and
HAVING HEARD the statements of the Secretary General of the Organization and the Permanent Representative of Haiti,
RESOLVES:
1.  To issue its most vigorous condemnation of those events and of their perpetrators, and to demand adherence to the Constitution and respect for the Government, which was legitimately established through the free expression of the will of that country's people.
2. In keeping with the principles of the OAS Charter and of the Santiago Commitment to democracy, to reaffirm its solidarity with the Haitian people in their struggle to strengthen their democratic system without foreign interference and in the exercise of their inalienable sovereign will.
3. To deplore the loss of human lives; to demand that those responsible be punished; and to demand that, in strict observance of international law, those parties put an end to the violation of the Haitian people's rights, respect the life and physical safety of President Jean-Bertrand

Aristide, and restore the President's exercise of his constitutional authority.

4. Considering the graveness of the events that have occurred in Haiti, to convene an ad-hoc Meeting of Ministers of Foreign Affairs pursuant to resolution AC/RES. 1080 (XXI-0/91), and to instruct the Secretary General to that effect.

On the morning of October 2, 1991, *The Washington Post* ran an editorial calling for a peacekeeping force for Haiti. The pertinent parts were as follows:

> Haiti's government has once again been overthrown by violence, but this time it's different. This time the expelled president, Jean-Bertrand Aristide, has been elected under a democratic constitution. That makes it essential to reverse this coup and return President Aristide to office. . . .
>
> A peacekeeping force is going to be required. That is the first item that the OAS needs to consider. Many OAS countries have forces capable of the job. Venezuela is a good friend of Haiti. Canada has French-speaking troops. Because the United States occupied Haiti for 19 years earlier in this century, it can't send soldiers. But it can support those who do. . . .
>
> Without an effective force in the country to preserve order, Haiti's democracy will be lost and with it, the Haitian people's last hope for a decent life.

The ad hoc Meeting of Ministers of Foreign Affairs which was recommended by the Permanent Council began at 5:00 pm, October 2, 1991. President Aristide gave the Ministers a detailed account of the coup. He gave thanks to the French and American ambassadors for their support during the ordeal. He revealed that the batallion guarding the palace had been willing to resist the military in rebellion but said he could not give the order for the killing of Haitians by Haitians. Aristide said that during his months in office, Lt. Gen. Raoul Cédras had been successful in hiding his dream to be president. He recommended that a delegation be sent to Haiti to explain the condemnation of the coup by the Organization of American States and measures already taken, which could be intensified.

U.S. Secretary of State James Baker endorsed Aristide's call for a mission to Haiti. By sending such a mission, led by the Secretary General, he said, "we would send an important message to those who have taken power in Haiti, as well as to the Haitian people."

If these steps do not succeed, he said "we must consider additional steps," but he did not specify what they might be. Nevertheless he was firm in saying "this coup will not succeed. . . . This Organization . . . must not, and I am sure will not rest, until the people of Haiti regain their democracy."

His words were reassuring and set the tone for the constructive discussion that followed.

In the early morning hours of October 3, the ad hoc meeting approved two resolutions. The first of these (MRE/RES 1/91) called for the Secretary General of the Organization, together with a group of Foreign Ministers from the Member States, "to go to Haiti immediately to inform those who hold power illegally that the American states reject the disruption of constitutional order and to advise them of decisions taken by this meeting."

The second resolution (MRE/RES 2/91) called for the formation of a civilian mission, to be known as OEA-DEMOC, to reestablish and strengthen constitutional democracy in Haiti. It would go to that country "to facilitate the reestablishment and strengthening of democratic institutions, the full force and effect of the Constitution and respect for the human rights of all Haitians; also to support the administration of justice and the adequate functioning of all institutions that will make it possible to achieve these objectives."

## The OAS Mission to Haiti

Lt. Gen. Cédras broadcast that he would receive the OAS mission but would not comply with the group's demand to reinstate Aristide. The mission arrived on October 4, led by OAS Secretary General Joao Baena Soares and composed of the Foreign Ministers of Argentina, Bolivia, Canada, Costa Rica, Trinidad and Tobago, Jamaica and Venezuela and for the United States, the Assistant Secretary of State for Inter-American States, Bernard Aronson.

The mission held two days of meetings with Cédras, October 4 and 5, overnighting in Kingston, Jamaica. Cédras denied that he was head of government and in a position to make decisions with respect to the mission's demands, including the return of Aristide. Among the mission members, Argentina and Venezuela took the hardest line against the military but the mission as a whole made no progress and returned to Washington empty-handed on October 6.

On October 7, as if to thumb his nose at the OAS, Cédras allowed the Haitian parliament building to be surrounded by military forces who obliged the lawmakers to approve the coup which had deposed President Aristide and to name Joseph Nerette, a Supreme Court Justice, provisional president of Haiti. He was sworn in the next day.

In summary, the OAS reacted rapidly to try to restore President Aristide and democracy to Haiti in the week following his overthrow but failed miserably to achieve any results.

## Embargo and Sanctions

At an OAS Foreign Ministers meeting on October 8, a unanimous resolution was passed urging all members to proceed immediately to freeze Haitian government assets and impose an embargo on trade with Haiti except for humanitarian aid (mostly food and medicine) delivered by international and private agencies. The intention of the resolution was to place pressure on the Haitian military to resume negotiations with the OAS mission to arrange for the return of President Jean-Bertrand Aristide to his legitimate post.

The resolution declared that Aristide was replaced illegally and stated that "no government that may result from this illegal situation will be accepted."

U.S. State Department spokesperson Margaret Tutwiler said "We do not accept the parliament's forced action as a legitimate constitutional reform. We will continue to work within the OAS to restore constitutional government and the return of President Aristide."

Unilaterally, the United States had already blocked all U.S. licences for exports to Haiti since October 2 and all financial transactions with the Haitian government since October 4.

In response to the generalized OAS embargo, some Haitian business leaders withdrew their support for the coup leaders and called for Aristide's conditional return to power. The assembly industries in Haiti, geared specifically to import-export trade, were brought to a halt, and some businessmen were making plans to move their production facilities to neighboring countries. It was estimated that the embargo had cost 65,000 jobs and that five to six family members depended on the meager earnings of each assembly worker.

On October 11, the UN General Assembly adopted a symbolic resolution that "strongly" condemned the Haitian coup but stopped short of asking the member states to adopt economic sanctions. However, it did demand full restoration of Aristide and appealed to members to take measures in support of resolutions of the Organization of American States, which of course, had just imposed a severe embargo and severe sanctions on Haiti. Stronger action was not possible because many Third World countries had military governments of their own and feared the vote might set a precedent for similar action against their regimes in the future.

In Haiti, provisional president Joseph Nerette appointed Jean-Jacques Honorat, a leader of the Haitian Center for Human Rights and a long-time foe of Aristide, to be prime minister, replacing Rene Preval, who had been appointed by Aristide. At the United Nations, Haitian Ambassador Fritz Longchamps, commented: "I don't see how the champion of human rights could be prime minister in this government of criminals and drug traffickers."

As if to prove this point Honorat warned that Aristide would be a "dead duck" if he returned to Haiti and predicted that Haiti would erupt in civil war if the United States and other countries carried out a trade embargo.

But the embargo was already functioning. Venezuela, main supplier of oil to Haiti, blocked all future shipments. Electricity was out in many provincial towns and cities. A strong demand for the dollar resulted in the devaluation of the Haitian gourde. International relief organizations began to suspend their operations. An international noose was tightening around the neck of an already impoverished nation.

U.S. Ambassador to Haiti Alvin P. Adams warned the 10,000 Americans living in Haiti that the country was on the verge of an emergency that could surpass any crisis in modern Haitian history. At the end of October the U.S. State Department ordered all but 30 embassy employees to leave the country.

Many Americans and other foreigners living in Haiti were missionaries or development specialists involved with hundreds of health, agricultural and humanitarian projects operating in the country. If they left, Haiti would lose its basic life net. Ironically, though the military and wealthy elite were most vocal in protesting the disastrous effect of the embargo on the poor, the poor were its strongest supporters. They felt it was the only hope for the return of the man they worshipped.

## *The Issue of Haitian Refugees*

Inevitably, as a result of the embargo and military oppression, life in Haiti became unbearable. The most desperate sold their property and used the money to purchase passage on boats that might be seaworthy enough to take them to the shores of Florida. At first the exit was a trickle, but by the end of 1991, 7,891 boat people, by count of the U.S. Coast Guard, had been intercepted on the high seas.

Early in November 1991, as the number of refugees began to increase, the U.S. Coast Guard began to return the Haitians to their own land. President Bush defended the policy as a means of deterring Haitians from risking their lives at sea. This policy was roundly denounced by members of Congress, human rights activists and the UN High Commissioner for refugees. A 1967 international convenant to which the United States is a signatory forbids the return of refugees to a place where they may be persecuted. On November 20, 1991, a federal judge in Miami ordered the Bush administration to stop returning Haitian refugees to Haiti. But the ruling was appealed, and the policy of forced repatriation was continued.

The sea journey from the coast of Haiti to the coast of Florida was perilous. The handmade craft were generally overloaded, ill-equipped, unsafe, with insufficient food, water, gasoline and other supplies. Storms swept many overboard. Others became seasick. The chances of reaching the Florida coast were virtually nil, if only because of the watchful Coast Guard. On November 21, 1991, twenty-three Haitians were reported drowned and over 100 more were presumed dead after a boat loaded with refugees capsized off the eastern coast of Cuba.

President Bush reluctantly changed his policy of returning Haitian refugees to Haiti and began to take them to United States-controlled Guantanamo Bay Naval Base in Cuba.

## *The Cartagena Meeting*

After four days of intense negotiations with leaders of the Haitian National Assembly in mid-November 1991, an OAS delegation to Haiti, led by Augusto Ramirez Ocampo, former Foreign Minister of Colombia, opened a door to the possible restoration of Aristide.

The legislative leaders agreed to meet with representatives of President Aristide to discuss the present crisis, but declined to commit themselves in advance to his return. The armed forces pledged to respect any agreement that might emerge.

The talks began in Cartagena, Colombia on November 23. Aristide, himself, attended. Discussion began on a cordial note but it was soon evident that the lawmakers, fearful of the reaction of Haiti's military leaders, would never agree to Aristide's return under any circumstances.

On the second day, the legislators went on the offensive and pressed for relaxation of the OAS-imposed embargo. But Ramirez made it clear that the OAS would not lift the embargo unless concrete steps were taken toward Aristide's return.

Aristide took the position that the embargo should be lifted only after he was permitted to name a new prime minister in consultation with the National Assembly. The lawmakers rejected this demand, insisting that the embargo be scrapped before any negotiations on the constitutional order could take place.

The only agreements were on the need for unspecified army reforms and the need to place the police under civilian authority; also on the necessity of resuming international aid to Haiti. The National Assembly negotiators would not even agree to recognize Aristide as the legitimate president of Haiti.

The talks had collapsed, but some diplomats found solace in the fact that the two sides in the dispute had at least talked to each other. A month before they had refused even to speak with one another.

Ramirez Campo remarked, "you can't resolve such a complicated, confrontational situation in one day in one city in view of the degree of belligerence that exists in the hearts of these people, the passion, and a long history of violence."

As Christmas approached, Aristide displayed a change of heart. He agreed to accept his long-time enemy René Theodore, head of Haiti's Communist Party, as Prime Minister, as a first step that could lead to his return to power.

# Chapter IV

# A Most Frustrating Year — 1992

The year 1992 was not a happy one for Haiti nor for the accomplishment of U.S. objectives in Haiti. The chances for Aristide's return were bleaker than ever. The problem of refugees leaving the island became more troublesome because of their overwhelming numbers and controversies over the way they were handled. The tightening of the embargo made the poor poorer and the rich richer. The army refused to compromise with Aristide and atrocities against his supporters multiplied in number and kind. Disease and unemployment increased, and the November 1992 U.S. presidential election created uncertainties as to future U.S. policies toward the beleaguered island republic.

A month by month analysis of the major events of the year follows:

## *January, 1992*

A stalemate developed with respect to Aristide's return to Haiti. Under an agreement arranged by the OAS, Aristide and René Theodore were to meet in Washington, D.C. to work out an arrangement whereby Aristide would name Theodore prime minister of Haiti and guide the nation through an interim period leading to Aristide's return. But neither Theodore nor leaders of the Haitian National Assembly, whose approval was also necessary, appeared.

Theodore, it seems, could not get army or parliamentary approval for the plan unless he was able to win concessions from the OAS such as lifting the embargo. As it turned out, the OAS at that moment was moving in the opposite direction. Its Secretary General, Joao Banena Soares, was contemplating calling a meeting of OAS Foreign Ministers to extend it.

Aristide, who did come for the meeting, refused to endorse the OAS proposal unless Theodore met with him, publicly acknowledged his (Aristide's) primacy as president of Haiti, denounced the coup, and agreed to the dismissal of Lt. Gen. Raoul Cédras and other officers involved in the coup. In addition, said Aristide, Theodore would have to agree on the date for his (Aristide's) return, on members of the cabinet and a reform program for the nation. Aristide was willing to grant amnesty to non-commissioned officers involved in the coup but said that Cédras and those allied with him must face going to jail or leave the country.

A week later, in Haiti, Theodore was the target of a police attack at a political meeting he was chairing. His bodyguard was killed and the attackers forced the politicians to the floor and kicked and beat them. Theodore was fortunate to escape. He said later that the attack called into question the ability of the government to maintain public order. Since he was awaiting parliamentary confirmation as Prime Minister, the question arose as to whether the attack was motivated by his plan to meet with Aristide in Washington.

The U.S. Department of State strongly condemned the attack and called U.S. Ambassador Adams to "discuss the incident's implications for U.S. policy."

As the month ended, the U.S. Supreme Court cleared the way for the U.S. Coast Guard to forcibly return 10,000 refugees to Haiti. About 9,800 refugees were at Guantanamo Bay and 2,000 on board cutters. In an emergency petition, the Bush administration argued that as many as 20,000 Haitians were preparing to leave their country and that a make-shift tent city at Guantanamo was already filled to capacity.

## *February, 1992*

The U.S. military began to repatriate refugees. An attorney for the Haitian Refugee Center in Miami called it a disgrace to send people back to a country that President Bush had called a totalitarian state. "We know that some of them are going to die," he said. But a spokesman for the Department of State said they had received no credible reports on reprisals on repatriated refugees.

On one occasion the U.S. Immigration Service did reverse itself. It allowed 41 Haitians to seek asylum who had previously been denied asylum, were returned to Haiti, and fled again after suffering threats and abuse. However, the Bush administration had not decided what to do with more than 200 Haitians at Guantanamo who were eligible for asylum but tested positive for HIV, the virus that causes AIDS. Aliens who test positive for HIV are not permitted to enter the United States, but in certain cases waivers may be given.

In both Haiti and the United States a debate waxed on whether to exempt export-import trade involving assembly plants in Haiti from the trade embargo. The argument against making the exemption was that doing so would give the signal that the United States had given up on trying to restore democracy to Haiti. OAS Secretary General Joao Baena Soares argued strongly that the United States should hang tough. The plan to relax this part of the embargo was greeted warmly by those assembly plant owners still in business, but seven out of 44 such industries had already closed permanently and 32 others had laid off most or all of their workers and were temporarily closed.

The meeting between Aristide and Theodore, aborted in January when Theodore failed to attend, was revived by the Organization of American States. The plan was the same: Theodore would be named Prime Minister and would serve as head of government for an interim period before Aristide would return to Haiti. This time, however, key members of the National Assembly participated in the discussions.

Aristide and Theodore had three days of fruitful meetings. They agreed to form a commission to draft a protocol for implementing their plan. The commission would be composed of two supporters of Aristide, two representatives of the OAS and two representatives of the National Assembly.

The main provisions of what became known as the Washington Agreement were as follows:

1. The agreement called for Aristide to return to Haiti without specifying a date and promised a general amnesty for all those involved in the coup which ousted him.
2. Theodore would be ratified as prime minister by the National Parliament and he would name a new cabinet endorsed by Aristide.
3. The OAS in turn would lift its economic embargo of the island republic, monitor human rights, help bolster Haiti's democratic institutions and coordinate a humanitarian relief program.

4.  In a concession, Aristide, who had long insisted that Gen. Raoul Cédras be removed as a condition for his return to power, accepted a formula that would at least temporarily maintain Cédras as chief of the 7,000-member armed forces.
5.  Aristide agreed with Senate President Dejean Belizaire, a chief rival and coup supporter, to respect "all decisions" taken by the National Assembly since the coup. (The National Assembly in October 1991 ratified Cédras in his post as commander-in-chief of the armed forces.)
6.  The agreement allowed for Aristide or others to challenge acts by the National Assembly by appealing to a reconciliation commission, to be appointed by Aristide, Belizaire, Medard, the president of the National Assembly and the president of the Electoral College.
7.  The pact must be approved by the National Assembly.
8.  Aristide and Theodore agreed to meet every two weeks to assess the progress of the government and the conditions for Aristide's return.

Aristide designated René Theodore to replace Jean-Jacques Honorat as provisional prime minister. Then, on February 23, he along with Theodore, Belizaire and Medard, signed the agreement, with OAS officials present, in the office of OAS Secretary General Joao Baena Soares.

OAS diplomats hailed the accord as an essential first step toward stabilizing the country and normalizing its ties abroad. One OAS official praised the agreement as "a tremendous change, and a victory for democracy." For the first time, he said, you had the government-in-exile and the parliament working together. In agreeing to respect the will of parliament, even provisionally, Aristide and the top law makers had reached an understanding that would enable the country's elected leadership and Cédras to save face.

The Bush administration urged all factions in Haiti's political crisis — particularly the military — to adhere to the agreement. U.S. Assistant Secretary of State Bernard Aronson, said the administration fully supported the agreement, which he called "an important step forward toward the resolution of Haiti's crisis. All individuals and institutions in Haiti, particularly the military, have a profound obligation to support the agreement and not obstruct it."

But the question remained, would the army let the plan go forward? There was still strong resistance in Haiti among the military to Aristide's return under any conditions. Neither members of the armed forces nor the provisional government in power had been present at the talks.

Although the accord was termed "a definite solution" to Haiti's crisis, there was some doubt among diplomats as to whether Haiti's de facto regime under provisional prime minister Honorat would accept Aristide's return. Honorat's own foreign minister said the government did not support the OAS talks.

About 2,000 anti-Aristide demonstrators protested outside the National Assembly carrying placards denouncing the OAS agreement. The organizer, Vladimir Jeanty, predicted that the lawmakers who signed the agreement, including Senate President Belizaire and Alexandre Medard, president of the legislature, would be arrested when they returned to Haiti.

In testimony before Congress, U.S. Secretary of State James Baker acknowledged that there was some question as to whether the accord would be acceptable to the military leadership and expressed the hope that the Haitian National Assembly would soon meet to ratify it.

Cédras indicated before the talks began that he would abide by any agreement made, but there was some question about Cédras' control over, or will to control, the armed forces. Indeed, the very meeting that had just concluded almost did not take place because a group of soldiers, presumably acting on their own, nearly prevented Theodore from boarding the plane that took him to Washington. Only after U.S. and Canadian embassy officials intervened was he permitted to board the aircraft.

An official army communique issued on February 24 provided some grounds for optimism. It called on all Haitians "to control their passions so that all social and political problems might be solved by dialogue and not violence."

Within 24 hours of signing the agreement, Aristide reneged on one of its major provisions. He indicated it was his intention to violate the provision to grant amnesty to all those involved in the coup when he told reporters that his opposition to an amnesty for General Cédras had not changed.

At the end of the month the U.S. Supreme Court rejected in an 8-1 vote a second and certainly final appeal to halt U.S. repatriation of refugees to Haiti.

February 7, 1992, the anniversary of Aristide's inauguration as president of Haiti, passed without celebrations.

## March, 1992

At first, conditions seemed favorable for parliamentary approval of the OAS-brokered agreement which would have ultimately restored President Aristide to Haiti under conditions which would have allowed him to exercise the full constitutional powers of that office. After all, the leaders of parliament had themselves signed the agreement. The Haitian Chamber of Commerce, in representation of the powerful business elite, gave its endorsement. Even more important, in view of the general feeling that the position of the military was the key factor for passage of the compromise by the National Assembly, a statement by army chief Raoul Cédras that the army would not take a stand on the issue raised hopes that the agreement would receive prompt parliamentary approval.

In a letter to René Theodore, Cédras reportedly wrote that the army would not open itself to criticism that it intended to influence the government in its debate over the plan. Theodore said that Cédras had personally assured him that he, Cédras, backed a negotiated settlement to the crisis. It appeared that all potential trouble spots were covered.

Within 10 days, this optimism had degenerated into pessimism. It was widely believed that there had been a heavy flow of money into the pockets of key members of the legislature. Possibly Cédras had been saying one thing in public and acting differently to sabotage the agreement behind the scenes.

At any rate, the first significant resistance emanated from the army-installed provisional government. Interim President Joseph Nerette delivered a defiant speech condemning the accord, which he attributed to "meddling foreigners."

"They want me to resign," he said, "but I won't give up if it means abandoning my country to all those with unhealthy ambitions."

Acting Prime Minister Jean-Jacques Honorat appointed a three-member commission to bargain the government's fate with parliamentary leaders and report back — *after three weeks!* This was obviously a delaying tactic, but the legislature accommodated the government by postponing a vote on ratification for one week. During this period, government-controlled radio and television campaigned to discredit both the agreement and its supporters. Reynold Georges, a former senator and adviser to Nerette, declared on national television that "the fact of having signed this agreement is akin to being caught red-handed violating the constitution, and the police or the army can arrest the guilty members of parliament without warrant or further ado."

Cédras gave his personal assurance to diplomats and lawmakers that the army would provide protection for members of parliament when they voted on the accord, but there was some question of his being able, or even wanting to control rank-and-file soldiers.

In exile, President Aristide did not help his cause by reminding everyone that Cédras was responsible for some 2,000 deaths during the violence which followed the 1991 coup, and by claiming that the constitution did not give him the power to grant amnesty for "crimes of blood," even though he had agreed to such an amnesty when he had signed the OAS agreement.

The legislature again postponed its vote, and finally asked the Haitian Supreme Court to rule on the constitutionality of the accord and the ratification procedure. When, on March 27, the Supreme Court ruled unanimously that the agreement was unconstitutional, the death of this noble effort was sealed.

## *April, 1992*

In a non-binding resolution, the OAS appealed to its 34 member states and other governments to halt all commercial and financial transactions with Haiti until Aristide was restored to office, and President Bush issued an order banning all U.S. firms and individuals from trading with Haiti until Aristide was restored.

U.S. officials in Puerto Rico made their first seizure of a ship under the embargo when it took possession of a tanker which had delivered 250,000 gallons of diesel fuel to Haiti. Interim Haitian Prime Minister Jean-Jacques Honorat swore in his new cabinet and said foreigners would have no more say in resolving Haiti's constitutional crisis.

A new wave of boat people, estimated at 3,400, left Haiti in the three-week period following the collapse of the OAS agreement, bringing the total of Haitians picked up by the U.S. Coast Guard since the September 30, 1991 coup to about 20,000. The U.S. Supreme Court ruled that the U.S. Government could resume, at least temporarily, returning some Haitians to their homeland.

On April 19, the U.S. Department of State revoked the visas of 20 prominent Haitians who had supported the military coup that deposed President Aristide. As the month came to an end *The New York Times* reported that U.S. diplomats in Haiti were expressing growing exasperation as their efforts to reverse the military coup had either backfired or had been ignored by forces opposed to the return of the Rev. Jean-Bertrand Aristide to his elected post.

## *May, 1992*

The OAS toughened the embargo against Haiti. Conditions in Haiti worsened and the exodus of refugees reached record proportions. Facilities at Guantanamo, Cuba reached their capacity of 12,500. The U.S. Coast Guard began refusing to pick up boatloads of Haitians fleeing their country unless their vessels were judged in imminent danger of sinking. President Bush announced that, henceforth, the U.S. would return all Haitian boat people directly to Haiti without considering them for refugee status. The new policy came under criticism as a violation of international law and of a 1981 treaty with Haiti. The numbers of refugee boats declined sharply. U.S. officials pointed out that Haitians could apply for political asylum at the U.S. Embassy in Port-au-Prince, but few were willing to do so because of surveillance by the Haitian police. At least a dozen countries in Europe, South America and Africa ignored the embargo. It cost an estimated 150,000 jobs in Haiti. It was estimated that for each job lost, at least six dependents suffered.

## *June, 1992*

Dozens of people were arrested and beaten and some were forced to walk naked in the streets after a military barracks near Cayes in southern Haiti was set fire. The crackdown claimed more than a dozen lives. Haiti's military-backed administration appointed a rival of Aristide, conservative economist, Marc Bazin, "consensus" premier, rebuffing international efforts to restore Aristide to power. The OAS rejected his appointment. Acting Prime Minister Jean Jacques Honorat and Acting President Joseph Nerette stepped down and Bazin assumed the powers of both positions. The presidency was left vacant indefinitely.

The General Accounting Office of the U.S. Congress reported that the OAS embargo against Haiti was being circumvented by nations in Europe and Africa and a few in Latin America.

Haitian police clubbed and arrested at least a dozen peaceful mourners in a funeral procession for Georges Ismery, brother of Antoine Izmery, who gave heavy financial backing to Aristide in 1990.

## *July, 1992*

A deadlock developed. The army would not allow Bazin to recognize Aristide as president, while Aristide insisted that he was constitutionally elected and had a right to that office. Bazin presented himself as an honest broker between the army and Aristide, but it was evident that the army would not permit him to compromise. The army wanted the international embargo lifted but was not prepared to make the key concession necessary for its termination, namely, restoration of Aristide to the presidency.

The OAS condemned Bazin's appointment and refused to recognize his government or even answer his appeals for a dialogue, while the United States, at odds with France, its principal ally on the issue, pressed for negotiations. Aristide insisted that he could not abandon key provisions of the Haitian constitution which prohibit military intervention in politics.

## *August, 1992*

In a 7-2 decision, the U.S. Supreme Court allowed the Bush administration to continue repatriating Haitians without a hearing until it would have the opportunity to review that policy. The only Haitian refugees remaining in Guantanamo were 233 with the HIV virus, along with 59 of their relatives. Amnesty International accused Haiti's military of reestablishing the repressive structure of the Duvalier dictatorship. It also accused the United States of ignoring the existence of human rights abuses in Haiti and flouting international law by refusing to accept Haitian refugees. *The Washington Post* ran an article extremely critical of the treatment of Haitian refugees by the United States at Guantanamo. Randall Robinson, Executive Director of TransAfrica, and Benjamin Hooks Executive Director of the NAACP, co-authored a highly critical article of U.S. refugee policy in general.

# September, 1992

The OAS reached an agreement with President Aristide and army puppet prime minister Marc Bazin for the stationing of 18 OAS observers in Haiti as a means to helping reduce human rights violations. Four repatriated refugees were jailed on charges of organizing an illegal attempt to smuggle Haitians to the United States. A spokesman for the U.S. Embassy said that the Haitian immigration police were making the arrests to stop boat-lift organizers from swindling migrants. An aide to Aristide strongly criticized the Bush administration for repatriating Haitians who could face persecution.

# October, 1992

A year after the violent overthrow of Aristide, his supporters and the military that ousted him remained in entrenched positions that made bleak his chances of returning to power. There was also consensus that the trade embargo had outlived its usefulness. But Prime Minister Bazin was unable to persuade the army to make concessions that would justify lifting the measure. Aristide succeeded in depriving him of legitimacy in the eyes of the international community. The result was the same type of stalemate that existed the day Aristide was overthrown. The poor were poorer and the rich were richer. Haiti lost 150,00 jobs, and commerce declined by 67 percent. Tuberculosis, malaria and typhoid were increasing. Nearly 38,000 persons had fled the island. Enough Haitians were living in the United States and other countries to form an invasion force, but during a political year, with the economy in poor condition and Democrats accusing Bush of overconcentration on foreign affairs to the neglect of domestic affairs, Bush felt he could not get further involved in Haitian affairs.

# November, 1992

Since President-elect Clinton promised to change Bush's policy of repatriating Haitian refugees without a hearing, the United States braced for a new wave of refugees after Inauguration Day. Fearing that President Clinton might be harder on them than Bush, Haitian military leaders offered to meet with Clinton representatives. The boat-building business boomed anew in Haiti. A November 17 speech by Clinton that he would do nothing to increase the refugee flow to the United States was not believed.

## December, 1992

A coalition of Haitian human rights organizations estimated that 3,000 political murders had occurred in Haiti since the September 1991 military coup. At Guantanamo, a group of 276 HIV-positive Haitians, including 42 children, continued to live in a barbed wire encampment, under inhumane conditions. Haitians found a new way to get into the United States — in cargo containers. U.S. intelligence estimated that 100,000 people were ready to depart on boats for the United States.

# Chapter V

# The Governors Island Agreement

A s 1993 opened, Haiti was caught on the horns of a dilemma. More numerous and more repulsive human rights violations by the police and military, coupled with promises by President-elect Clinton of a more liberal policy toward Haitian refugees, drove more Haitians to take to the sea in makeshift boats in search of freedom. The only solution to this dilemma lay in reconciliation between Aristide and the military, but this seemed more remote than ever. Aristide insisted on his constitutional rights, and the military vowed never to permit his return.

## *Enter Dante Caputo*

New hope developed as the United Nations began to take a more active interest in the Haitian problem. Previously content to listen to speeches from President Aristide and to take note of OAS resolutions, now, with an outpouring of up to 150,000 Haitian refugees foreseen, the United Nations and its agencies decided it should play a larger role. Dante Caputo, former Argentine foreign minister, was selected as the official OAS/UN representative for negotiations with Haiti's military rulers.

A wiser move could not have been made. The Haitian problem was broadened from a United States problem, or even an OAS problem, to an international problem, and as such received greater attention by more nations. No longer were unwieldy, multilateral missions sent out to seek solutions. One man embodied the interests of all nations, served all nations, and had the confidence of everyone involved.

Caputo was a skilled diplomat. He insisted that all agreements he reached be confirmed by letter. He recognized the obvious fact that restoration of democracy in Haiti was the key to solving the Haitian dilemma and worked diligently toward the achievement of that objective.

Caputo met with President-elect Clinton and his transition team. He also traveled around Haiti, talking to all factions, especially military and government leaders. He held out incentives for their cooperation, mainly lifting the embargo that was devastating the country. Of course the reverse was obvious even if unstated: no cooperation, no relief from the embargo, and possibly additional and better targeted sanctions.

The main actors in the drama began to rethink their positions. The U.S. Government began to recognize that the long term solution to the Haitian refugee problem was not so much how to cope with the refugees once they left their homeland but rather making Haiti a more attractive place for them to stay.

Aristide modified his position toward Lt. Gen. Raoul Cédras. "I do not wish to do vengeance," he said. "I do not think of putting him in jail or on trial. But I do think that, as symbol of the coup, he should be removed from power."

In *The Washington Post* he indicated a readiness to grant a general amnesty to the army at large; also, that "for the sake of building unity," he had agreed to name a member of the opposition to prime minister and to run the government. "I remain prepared to work with a prime minister of the opposition," he wrote, "in order to mend our shattered nation and begin the rebuilding."

President Aristide also made a broadcast in Creole to Haiti telling his people that President Clinton, the OAS and the United Nations were making great efforts to return democracy to Haiti and urging them not to undertake the perilous sea journey in a fruitless search for political asylum, but rather to resist within the country without violence until he was returned by the United States, the United Nations and the OAS.

Dante Caputo succeeded early in gaining the agreement of Lt. Gen. Raoul Cédras and Primer Minister Marc Bazin to the deployment of an international observer force of civil rights monitors in Haiti and the reopening of talks aimed at restoring democracy to that beleaguered nation. Since Aristide had already agreed to such talks, the way was clear for them to begin, he said, although it would take some time to make arrangements. Caputo said he had with him a letter from General Cédras to UN Secretary General Boutros Boutros-Ghali accepting the talks. He said that up to 400 OAS human rights monitors might soon arrive in Haiti. They would have an effect in reducing the outflow of refugees, he said, by diminishing the political violence in the country and thus the desire to leave.

The next and more difficult stage of his efforts, he said, would be to work out a framework for negotiations leading to the restoration of civilian democracy to the country.

Caputo told the OAS in Washington that he had emphasized to Haitian military leaders that "the world community will not stand for any result other than a full restoration of democracy, including the return of President Aristide to his rightful position."

He said the negotiations leading up to this ultimate objective would be difficult and could take several weeks. It would be difficult to begin this dialogue as long as Haiti was threatened with violence; therefore, he said, it was critical to get the human rights monitors to Haiti as soon as possible.

Unfortunately, Caputo was forced to return to Haiti when, to everyone's surprise, Prime Minister Marc Bazin announced that he would never sign the agreement for the human rights monitors. He said the proposed terms would place the nation under "international tutelage." He called the document a violation of Haiti's sovereignty, saying the mission gave itself the right to go anywhere freely and enter any establishment without being accompanied and without forewarning."

Bazin did say, however, that he accepted the principle of the mission and that he was forming a working group to analyze the document and make counterproposals.

On his arrival, Caputo was greeted at the airport with a violent government-orchestrated demonstration during which a prominent Haitian journalist was kidnapped. In new conversations with Caputo, Bazin presented him with amendments that would give the Haitian government considerable input with respect to the size and membership of the mission and the right to restrict its movements. Caputo considered these unacceptable but made no public statements. The U.S. embassy provided him with security during the entire visit.

Reaction of the United Nations and the U.S. and Canadian governments to these events was firm. UN Secretary General Boutros Boutros-Ghali condemned the harassment of his representative, Dante Caputo, and issued a four-day deadline for Bazin and Cédras to agree to the UN terms for the mission. UN officials said they were also considering expansion of the current OAS regional trade embargo to cover all nations. U.S. Secretary of State Warren Christopher said that the Clinton administration was considering economic sanctions on the Haitian military to compel cooperation with the UN/OAS effort. The response of Canadian Prime Minister Brian Mulroney was even stronger. "Personally, I feel that at the appropriate time we can take more hard action . . . we don't have the right to let stand a government which is crushing democracy, liberty and the personal rights and liberties of individuals." Clinton, who was standing next to him, said, "I share the prime minister's determination," and he promised "a more vigorous course" of action should current efforts fail. These positions were vigorously communicated to Bazin and Cédras over the weekend of February 6 and 7.

The first result was the return of Colson Dorme, the young Haitian radio news journalist, who had been kidnapped during the government-sponsored demonstration against Caputo. After a week, when many had given him up for dead, he suddenly surfaced, dumped near his radio station in his underwear, bound and bruised, his head shaven. When he came to his senses, he described six days of incessant beatings, interrogation under hot lights, and confinement, blindfolded, in a dingy secret prison. His captors had stolen his money and his tape recorder. He was the personification of the urgent need for international monitors of human rights in Haiti.

Two days later, on February 9, 1993, it was announced in New York, Washington and Port-au-Prince that Haitian authorities had agreed to allow a team of international human rights observers to operate in the country. A group of 40 OAS observers, including 15 Americans, and a few UN human rights experts would be leaving for Haiti within four days. These would complement the 16 OAS observers already in place, whose work had been severely circumscribed. The Mission was expected to grow to 200.

Prime Minister Marc Bazin said his government would cooperate with the mission if it stayed within its mandate and violated neither the Haitian Constitution nor Haitian sovereignty. Language to that effect was incorporated in the final accord.

UN officials said the military-backed government had endorsed a formal one-year agreement that allowed observers to travel unannounced, without escort, to any point within Haiti. It guaranteed the safety of the observers and pledged aid to them with communications. The United States agreed to contribute at least $2 million to the operation.

Even Aristide became conciliatory. He said that if the joint mission got underway and Caputo could certify that tangible progress on human rights was being made, then sanctions could be lifted gradually even before his return.

The UN/OAS mission arrived February 14, 1993 and passed its first test February 25 when a funeral mass for an estimated 600 to 900 people who had died in a ferry disaster turned into a large pro-Aristide demonstration. Bishop Willy Romelus, a prominent clergyman who gave the oration, was attacked by armed men when he left the cathedral. He was rescued when members of the UN/OAS mission jumped between the bishop and the attackers.

## *Coping with Refugees*

In the United States, attention was focused on the government's court battle to be allowed to continue its policy of repatriating refugees intercepted on the high seas.

President Clinton found himself in the unenviable position of having to decide whether to defend before the U.S. Supreme Court a Bush policy he had roundly criticized during the 1992 presidential campaign as being inhumane, immoral and illegal. In July 1992, when the 2nd Circuit Court of Appeals in New York ruled that the Bush policy violated both U.S. and international law, Clinton issued a statement saying that the court had made the right decision, and he condemned Bush for "a cruel policy of returning Haitian refugees to a brutal dictatorship." Now Clinton said he had changed his position and would defend the government's repatriation policy because he had been "profoundly moved by the loss of life of those fleeing Haiti in homemade boats."

Because Clinton had not yet gotten around to make the top appointments at the Department of Justice, the attorney who defended the government's policy was Deputy Solicitor General Maureen E. Mahoney, a civil servant. She argued the case with brilliance against some 150 civil rights lawyers, claiming that the President's power to control immigration is inherent in his power to establish U.S. foreign policy and in his obligation to defend the U.S. national interest. U.S. immigration and international law bar the government from returning a refugee to territories where his life or freedom would be threatened, but Ms. Mahoney successfully argued that these laws do not apply to persons outside U.S. territory. The government won its case and forced repatriation continued.

One group of refugees still presented a special problem. These were 215 refugees already accepted for political asylum who were HIV-infected or already had AIDS and were being held at the Guantanamo Naval Base, along with 52 of their relatives and dependents not affected by the AIDS virus. They had been detained a year in conditions of squalor while a legal battle over their fate moved slowly through court channels. U.S. law prohibits entry into the United States of persons with AIDS or HIV infection, although exceptions can be made. Finally, on March 27, 1993, a federal judge in New York gave the government 10 days to provide medical treatment for these refugees or to send them where they could receive treatment. They were sent to Miami, Florida, causing near panic among the people there and outrage in the U.S. Congress.

One refugee case deserves special attention for its uniqueness. A young Haitian navy deserter granted refugee status by the U.S. embassy was arrested at the airport by Haitian soldiers minutes before he was scheduled to board a plane for Miami. He was escorted by Haitian soldiers, and accompanied by a U.S. embassy official, to the army-operated National Penitentiary in Port-au-Prince. The Haitian military announced he would be court martialed.

President Clinton demanded his immediate release. Officials of the National Coalition for Haitian Refugees said his arrest had been ordered by General Cédras. The U.S. State Department saw it as a test case of the willingness of the Haitian regime to cooperate on military matters. Finally, three days after his detention, the military relented and permitted Seaman Coracelin to leave on a flight to New York.

Aristide, with half his term as president of Haiti completed, most of it in exile, met with President Clinton and asked him to set a definite date for the restoration of democracy in Haiti and for his return to power. President Clinton said he could not do so but assured Aristide that he was "committed strongly" to a much more aggressive effort to restore him to his position, and, over the long haul, to work with the people of Haiti to restore economic prosperity to the country.

## *Reconciliation?*

With 119 UN/OAS human rights monitors in place in Haiti, Dante Caputo, the UN/OAS negotiator for Haiti, turned to the second and more difficult part of his mission: to secure agreement from the Haitian military for the return of President Jean-Bertrand Aristide to his legitimate post on the island.

For weeks Caputo shuttled back and forth between Washington and Port-au-Prince, soliciting ideas and concessions from President Aristide and Lt. Gen. Raoul Cédras. He sought agreement from the de facto government to allow a 500-man international police force to be stationed in Haiti to help prepare the way for Aristide's return. The army had initially asked for the force to protect itself and agreed to it privately, then publicly repudiated the idea.

The United States retaliated by placing targeted sanctions on about 100 senior government officials and military officers, and on their families and financial supporters. The United States also froze the financial assets of 83 persons who were acting on behalf of the military, as well as the assets of the central bank and of three other financial institutions. These persons and institutions were banned from conducting commercial transactions in the United States. Among the persons hit by the new sanctions were General Cédras and Prime Minister Marc Bazin. It was the first time, after months of threats, that the United States had punished the illegal government for failure to meet international demands.

The Organization of American States passed a resolution stating that it was incumbent upon all the Haitian parties involved in the negotiations to take true responsibility for solving the crisis. The organization also pledged continuous support for their special envoy, Dr. Dante Caputo.

One immediate result of these sanctions was the resignation of Prime Minister Marc Bazin. He had often boasted of his financial connections in Washington but had failed to avert this financial disaster which had fallen on the leadership elements in Haiti, himself included. He lost the support of the army when he tried to replace four cabinet ministers, two of whom were appointees of the military.

Supporters of Aristide in Port-au-Prince rejected overtures by the military to cooperate in setting up a new civil government. They called instead for the resignation of the military leaders who had ousted their president. The Bazin cabinet ran the government while the politicians and the military sought to resolve their differences.

Human rights organizations reported that beatings, torture and extrajudicial executions were more common than under the worst times of the Duvalier dictatorships of 1957 to 1986.

Many of Aristide's followers, who had taken the international community at its word that the return of their leader was imminent, came out of hiding, were arrested and suffered cruel beatings. Human rights monitors in the countryside reported that victims were generally struck by small wooden batons and given 150 blows: 50 for being an Aristide supporter, 50 for being a member of a local peasant organization and 50 for the Organization of American States. They had to count the blows as they received them, and if they missed a number, they had to begin their count anew.

According to one monitoring report, one victim received about 750 blows, mostly to the buttocks, leaving them looking like raw meat with a crust of dry blood nearly an inch thick.

"As they beat him, they shouted 'Down with the OAS, down with MMP (the local peasant organization), down with Aristide,'" the report said. "They made him dance, and when he could not, they beat the bottoms of his feet. They told him he was lucky he was home; otherwise they would have beaten his wife because she was the one who was having substantial contacts with the (human rights) mission."

The army and their civilian helpers, called *attachés*, sometimes deliberately beat followers of Aristide in full view of human rights monitors to demonstrate that they could do so with impunity. According to their mandate, UN/OAS monitors were authorized to observe and report but not to intervene.

As reports circulated that the United Nations was on the verge of imposing a world-wide oil embargo on Haiti, Haiti's parliament recognized the legitimacy of President Aristide and asked him to name a new prime minister. But they imposed conditions on his return that his followers would not accept.

The military high command rejected an invitation to meet with representatives of Aristide under UN auspices in New York. Incredibly, in a letter to Caputo, Raoul Cédras said it would be "unconstitutional" for the army to become involved in politics. Aristide had accepted such talks as a framework for the resignation of the military leaders involved in the coup and the transfer of power to a civilian government.

On July 16, 1993, the United Nations Security Council voted unanimously to impose a worldwide oil and arms embargo on Haiti, along with a global freeze on the Haitian government's financial assets. The embargo would go into affect in seven days unless Haiti's military leaders talked with representatives of President Aristide in the interim and agreed in writing to a firm plan for his return as legal president of Haiti.

Dante Caputo said that the purpose of the sanctions was not just to punish the Haitian authorities but rather to bring them into negotiations for Aristide's return. Five days later General Raoul Cédras sent a letter to Caputo saying that he was willing to meet with Aristide. On June 24, 1993, Aristide agreed to such talks and Caputo announced that they would begin at 9 a.m., Sunday, June 27, at UN headquarters in New York. For reasons of greater privacy and greater security, the discussions took place at a U.S. Coast Guard base on Governors Island in New York harbor. Aristide and Cédras never met face to face. They were seated with their staffs at separate locations. Caputo shuttled back and forth between them with messages and suggestions. The outcome of five days of negotiations was a ten-point agreement as follows:

AGREEMENT OF GOVERNORS ISLAND
The President of the Republic of Haiti, Jean-Bertrand Aristide, and the Commander-in-Chief of the Armed Forces of Haiti, Lieutenant-General Raoul Cédras, have agreed that the following arrangements should be made in order to resolve the Haitian crisis. Each of them has agreed to take, within the scope of his powers, all the necessary measures for the implementation of these arrangements. Furthermore, they both, in any case, express their support for the implementation of these arrangements and pledge to cooperate in implementing them.

1.  Organization, under the auspices of the United Nations and the Organization of American States (OAS), of a political dialogue between representatives of the political parties represented in the Parliament, with the participation of representatives of the Presidential Commission, in order to: a) agree to a political truce and promote a social pact to create the conditions necessary to ensure a peaceful transition; b) reach an agreement on the procedure for enabling the Haitian Parliament to resume its normal functioning; c) reach an agreement enabling the Parliament to confirm the Prime Minister as speedily as possible; and d) reach an agreement permitting the adoption of the laws necessary for ensuring the transition.
2.  Nomination of a Prime Minister by the President of the Republic.
3.  Confirmation of the Prime Minister by the legally reconstituted Parliament and his assumption of office in Haiti.
4.  Suspension, on the initiative of the United Nations Secretary-General, of the sanctions adopted under Security Council resolution 841 (1993) and suspension, on the initiative of the Secretary-General of OAS, of the other measures adopted at the OAS Ad Hoc Meeting of Ministers of Foreign Affairs, immediately after the Prime Minister is confirmed and assumes office in Haiti.

5.  Implementation, following the agreements with the constitutional Government, of international cooperation: a) technical and financial assistance for development; b) assistance for the administrative and judicial reform; c) assistance for modernizing the Armed Forces of Haiti and establishing a new Police Force with the presence of United Nations personnel in these fields.
6.  An amnesty granted by the President of the Republic within the framework of article 147 of the National Constitution and implementation of the other instruments which may be adopted by the Parliament on this question.
7.  Adoption of a law establishing the new Police Force. Appointment, within this framework, of the Commander-in-Chief of the Police Force by the President of the Republic.
8.  The Commander-in-Chief of the Armed Forces of Haiti has decided to avail himself of his right to early retirement and the President of the Republic shall appoint a new Commander-in-Chief of the Armed Forces of Haiti, who shall appoint the members of the General Staff, in accordance with the Constitution.
9.  Return to Haiti of the President of the Republic, Jean-Bertrand Aristide, on 30 October 1993.
10. Verification by the United Nations and the Organization of the American States of fulfillment of all the foregoing commitments.

The President of the Republic and the Commander-in-Chief agree that these arrangements constitute a satisfactory solution to the Haitian crisis and the beginning of a process of national reconciliation. They pledge to cooperate fully in the peaceful transition to a stable and lasting democratic society in which all Haitians will be able to live in a climate of freedom, justice, security and respect for human rights.

_____                    _____

Jean-Bertrand Aristide                     Lieutenant-General Raoul Cédras
President of the                           Commander-in-Chief of the
Republic of Haiti                          Armed Forces of Haiti


Signed July 3, 1993

# Chapter VI

# The Harlan County Turns Tail

There were no celebrations after the signing of the Agreement of Governors Island, just sighs of relief and crossed fingers. Aristide was the aggrieved party in the dispute; he had been deposed in a military coup and had spent 21 months in exile. Cédras was the villain. Nevertheless, in an effort to act as honest broker, UN mediators actually placed more pressure on Aristide to make concessions than on Cédras, concessions that Aristide made with great reluctance and would soon come to regret. At one point, Dante Caputo announced that the conference would end on Saturday, July 3, regardless of the state of negotiations at that time. With the adoption of Point 4 lifting the sanctions on Haiti, Cédras had already achieved his principal objective. He signed the agreement separately early on July 3 and immediately left for Haiti.

## *The Agreement's Deficiencies*

In terms of both structure and substance, the Governors Island Agreement had many deficiencies. First and foremost, the lifting of the embargo was placed too early in the sequence of steps to be taken under the agreement. It should have been designated the final step. It was the embargo that had brought Cédras to the bargaining table. Its removal as the final step would have served as an incentive to, and reward for, rapid completion of the other steps.

Under the agreement Cédras pledged to "avail himself of his right to early retirement," but he was not pinned down to a specific date for such action in the text.

The retirement of Lt. Gen. Michel Francois, Chief of police, was not even mentioned in the agreement, though he was generally considered to have played the major role in the coup which ousted President Aristide and shared the guilt with Cédras for the thousands of atrocities committed against Aristide's supporters in the months that followed the coup.

The return of Aristide to Haiti should have been scheduled to take place much earlier in the sequence of steps, rather than at the very end. Cédras was free to continue his mischief for four months while Aristide languished in exile. Aristide's return should have been made to coincide with the retirement or reassignment of all high ranking officers involved in the coup and its bloody aftermath, so as to establish a clear break between the end of military rule and the reestablishment of civilian democracy. Indeed, a chronology with dates and deadlines should have been established throughout the text of the agreement, with provisions written in for reinstating the embargo if commitments were not fulfilled in timely fashion. In retrospect, it is obvious that Cédras had signed the agreement in order to buy time for himself and his military colleagues and had absolutely no intention of abiding by its terms.

Point 10 of the agreement called for verification of fulfillment of its terms by the United Nations and the Organization of American States but created no mechanism for accomplishing this task, nor for correcting violations or penalizing transgressions.

In the final words of the agreement, Aristide and Cédras pledged "to cooperate fully in the peaceful transition to a stable and lasting democratic society in which all Haitians will live in a climate of freedom, security and human rights."

Cédras broke his pledge within 10 days of affixing his signature to the agreement by ordering all OAS human rights monitors out of the country. The OAS felt it had no alternative but to comply and ordered its mission, which then numbered 104 members, to leave at once, which it did.

The UN Security Council passed a resolution declaring the expulsion "a serious escalation in the defiant stance of Haiti's illegal de facto regime toward the international community." which it was, but took no counteraction. The United States merely stated the obvious: "This provocative behavior affects the peace and security of the region." The United States, too, failed to take countermeasures, proving to all that Cédras could continue to defy the international community at will, without fear of retribution. It gave undue legitimacy to his illegal government and cleared the way for him and Francois to intensify their campaign of terror against Aristide's supporters.

# *Quick Initial Progress*

Nonetheless, quick initial progress was made on the first five points of the Governors Island Agreement. Caputo invited representatives of the main political forces in Haiti and of the political blocs in parliament to meet in New York to participate in a dialog aimed at creating the conditions to insure a peaceful transition to democracy in Haiti (Point 1). Their agreement became known as the New York Pact. Aristide nominated a respected businessman, Robert Malval, as Prime Minister of Haiti (Point 2). He was promptly confirmed by a reconstituted parliament and installed in the post at a ceremony organized by President Aristide in Washington (Point 3). One of his first acts was to ask the United Nations to suspend its sanctions on Haiti. This was done on August 27, 1993 (Point 4). In addition, as authorized under Point 5c of the Governors Island Agreement, the United Nations started working on plans to send 567 police monitors to Haiti from Canada, France and Venezuela for the purpose of training a new Haitian police force; also, a contingent of about 500 U.S. military engineers to help restore the basic infrastructure of the country. An additional 60 military trainers would help to build a professional army.

## *The Attachés Attack*

The forward progress did not continue for long. Shortly after Primer Minister Malval was installed with his cabinet in a ceremony at the National Palace on September 2, 1993, plainclothed police auxiliaries beat people with clubs to break up a group of about 150 persons chanting pro-Aristide slogans. On September 8, some 200 municipal employees of City Hall ran amok as Aristide's associate, Evans Paul, tried to return to his position as mayor of Port-au-Prince. One man was killed and 15 wounded in a rampage of civil servants armed with guns, staves and knives. Paul claimed that the attacks were carried out at the instigation of the army. The attackers were known as *attachés*, civilian auxiliaries licensed to carry guns in return for their assistance with police work and political repression. Their rewards came from permission to steal from their victims. They were estimated to number in the tens of thousands.

Paul went into hiding for fear of his life. He summed up his dilemma accurately when he said, "It is one thing to have legal power and another thing to exercise it. We do not have a public force which obeys us." In other words the military and police dictatorship was dominant over the civilian government.

On September 11, 1993, a highly respected businessman, Antoine Izmery, a close friend of Aristide, was dragged from a church in Port-au-Prince and assassinated. An unidentified gunman sauntered down the aisle, grabbed him, and together with about a dozen accomplices, forced him to the street and shot him in the head. A few hours later, a retired army colonel, Antoine Jocelyn, was killed by a gunman in the fashionable suburb of Petitionville.

UN/OAS special envoy Dante Caputo linked Police Chief Lt. Col. Michel Francois to these and the wave of more than 100 other killings that had taken place in the city during the months following the signing of the Governors Island Agreement. There were, of course, no UN/OAS human rights monitors to investigate these murders. Private international rights organizations estimated an additional 30 "disappearances." Of these, 19 reappeared, the private monitors said, and they reported having been interrogated and tortured. They attributed much of this violence to the government's security apparatus.

Parliament was deadlocked, and Prime Minister Malval and his cabinet were helpless in their attempts to control this reign of terror. Malval was obliged to work from his home because officials of the military government refused to vacate the premises he chose to use outside the presidential palace, then undergoing repair. He issued orders to the police which were always ignored. Despite demands by the transition government that the attachés be disarmed, more and more of them were recruited and trained for vile acts of terror and intimidation. Thousands of rural sheriff deputies also formed part of this apparatus, as well as an estimated 30,000 thugs who suddenly appeared, all former members of the *Tonton Macoutes* of the Duvalier era.

Obviously the army's aim was to create such havoc and instability that Aristide could not be returned safely, and to convince everyone that the Haitian army, and only the Haitian army, was capable of maintaining internal security.

Thus was the climate in Haiti six weeks before Aristide's scheduled return as president of the nation.

## *Rebuff of the Harlan County*

On September 23, 1993, the UN Security Council voted to send more than 1,200 police and military advisers to Haiti under terms of the Governors Island Agreement. The contingent would include 500 uniformed Americans. Their purpose would be to help stabilize the country before the scheduled return of President Aristide on October 30.

Most of the U.S. troops would be Navy engineers who would train the Haitian army in road-building and other civic action. U.S. officers would train Haitian troops on the role of the military in a democratic society. The police monitors would come primarily from France, Canada and Nigeria. They would be stationed at posts around the nation to train and monitor the Haitian police. They would not be authorized to use force or to perform police functions. They would also serve to discourage reprisals by Aristide supporters on the national army and police.

On September 30, the first U.S. navy vessel, with about 250 linguists, medical specialists and military trainers, left Norfolk for the Caribbean. A senior Pentagon official emphasized that this would be a nation-building effort conducted with permission of the new Haitian government. Nevertheless one squadron of military police was included in the deployment.

The ship, loaded with construction equipment, would pick up dozens of "Seabees", from naval battalions in Puerto Rico. They would arrive in Port-au-Prince on October 11, 1993.

Obviously General Cédras was aware of the day and hour of their arrival. Early that morning he made a point to lay a wreath at the foot of the statue of General Jean-Jacques Dessalines, commander of the forces that had led Haiti to independence in 1804. Dessalines was a fierce and unforgiving warrior who ordered his troops to cut heads and burn houses in the life or death struggle against the French. The wreath laying ceremony set the tone for the day's events.

As a contingent of 193 U.S. and 25 Canadian soldiers approached a dock in Port-au-Prince aboard the tank landing ship USS Harlan County, a chanting crowd of about 100 armed persons gathered on the wharf, with open police support, chanting anti-U.S. slogans. Several ships blocked the dock, making it impossible for the Harlan County to unload. When Vicki Huddleston, U.S. charge d'affaires, arrived to welcome the soldiers, the crowd gathered around her vehicle and those of other diplomats, refused to let them enter the dock area, and shouted threats. The protestors banged on their cars and rocked them as uniformed police looked on, doing nothing to stop them. Shots were fired into the air as they left, panicking passersby and sending scores of people looking for shelter.

A larger crowd of several hundred persons carrying the red and black flag of the former Duvalier dictatorship set up barricades along the main streets and shouted that they would burn all foreigners. They chanted, "this is no joke, this is no joke, they will not take over our country."

Police in dark glasses helped direct a busload of armed plain clothesmen to parking places outside the locked dock gates, and uniformed soldiers in government trucks snaked through the crowds. The protesters were led by known supporters of the brutal Duvalier dictatorships. They took over the state radio station and urged listeners to "come to the port now, so the foreigners can see we are not just a small group of recalcitrants."

Prime Minister Malval and his cabinet had planned to hold a welcoming ceremony, but decided to cancel it. The Harlan County, a 560-foot flat bottom ship with no combat capability, anchored in the harbor about half a mile from shore.

A senior aide to Malval said that the protestors were "scum" and were waging "psychological warfare" to persuade the international community that their troops were as unsafe in Haiti as in Somalia.

"It is a show for the Americans," he said, "to tell the Americans this is Somalia, but it is not. This is a problem of gangs. They could be controlled if the army wanted to, but if the army does not want to cooperate, the government cannot take control by itself.

At a news conference at the U.S. Embassy, Huddleston said that those who carried out the day's actions were a group of gangsters, a group of thugs, who don't want the future of Haiti to arrive.

At the same news conference Dante Caputo, UN/OAS mediator, said, "Today we have seen a clear violation of the commitments taken by the Haitian armed forces."

In a brief statement read to reporters, Cédras condemned the violence but said that new questions had been raised about the legality of foreigners on Haitian soil. He said he had asked Parliament and the Supreme Court to rule on the validity of the international force.

In retrospect, it can be asserted that the landing of the Harlan County had not been well-planned and that U.S. intelligence on the mood, plans and capabilities of resistance elements was either non-existent or faulty.

The question also arises, why did the United States and the United Nations, who had been waiting for years for the departure of Cédras and Francois, not wait just four days more, until October 15, when Cédras was scheduled to resign and Francois scheduled to take a diplomatic post? Or perhaps until October 30, when Aristide was scheduled to return to Haiti, and the planned and necessary engineering and reform projects could have been conducted in a friendlier atmosphere?

There is no question that the Harlan County rebuff was a major embarrassment to the United States and sowed doubt worldwide on U.S. capacity to carry out its foreign policy commitments.

# Chapter VII

# Groping for a Solution

Both on and off the island, the rebuff of the Harlan County was widely interpreted as a victory for the military leadership of Haiti. It brought progress on the Governors Island Agreement to a standstill. A second ship, the USS Fairfax County, had been scheduled to leave Virginia for Haiti the following week on an identical mission, but its departure was immediately canceled. In Haiti chargé d'affaires Vicki Huddleston met with General Cédras for three hours but could not persuade him to recommit himself to accepting and protecting a military training mission as called for in the Governors Island Agreement which he had signed just three months before.

It was learned that the angry mob that prevented the Harlan County from landing its troops was composed of members of a paramilitary organization called the Front for the Advancement and Progress of Haiti, or FRAPH, from its acronym in French, which roughly means "to strike." It was set up by prominent members of the Duvalier dictatorships who had recently returned from exile. Both Police Chief Michel Francois and Lt. Gen. Cédras, sons of prominent Duvalier supporters, welcomed their return. They had been given as their first major assignment, frustration of the Harlan County landing.

Hubert de Ronceray, prominent anti-Aristide legislator, supported by former members of the Duvalier dictatorship, demanded formal cancellation of the Governors Island accord. In a letter to Caputo, Cédras said that the agreement "appears to be dead."

As tension mounted the Canadian embassy urged its citizens to leave on commercial flights, and the U.S. Embassy asked Americans to register in case an evacuation became necessary.

## *Much Talk, Little Action*

President Clinton called for the resumption of economic sanctions against Haiti. "I want the Haitians to know that I'm dead serious about seeing them honor the agreement they made," he said.

The United Nations voted to reimpose its sanctions against Haiti within five days unless the military leaders stopped violating their commitments under the agreement, signed under UN auspices.

At a news conference in Port-au-Prince, Cédras said that he would step down "tomorrow" if the Haitian parliament would approve a general amnesty for him and others accused in the 1991 coup. "I am ready to resign for the good of the nation." he said. Asked if that would be by October 15, the deadline he had previously set for himself, he answered softly, "I hope."

The UN Security Council voted unanimously on October 13 to reimpose its oil embargo on Haiti and to freeze the financial assets of military leaders involved in blocking the arrival of the Harlan County. UN Secretary General Boutros Boutros-Ghali identified Cédras and Port-au-Prince Police Chief Lt. Col. Michel Francois as having failed to honor their promises.

The Secretary General reported that all necessary commitments had been obtained in writing from the military and port authorities for the soldiers to disembark. Nevertheless he said, the port was blocked, and the authorities denied having had any contact with United Nations representatives. Despite repeated appeals to Cédras and Francois, Boutros-Ghali said, nothing was done to bring the situation under control.

U.S. Ambassador Madeline K. Albright said Washington would impose its own financial and travel restrictions on about 100 Haitian military officers and their civilian supporters.

There was no question that the opponents of the return of President Aristide were much emboldened by their success in preventing the Harlan County from accomplishing its mission.

## *Conditions Worsen*

On October 14, Haiti's Minister of Justice Francois Guy Malary, a highly respected lawyer educated at Georgetown and Howard Universities in Washington, D.C., was gunned down, along with his driver and one of his bodyguards, when bullets riddled his government-issued Toyota Land Cruiser outside the Justice Ministry. He was part of the transition government installed September 2 to pave the way for the return of President Aristide. He had been leading a legislative initiative to separate the Haitian police from the army. It was not clear who was responsible for the slayings, but many ministers of the transition government had received death threats from civilian gunmen, known as *attachés*, linked to the police and army. Malary's wife arrived on the scene, took his wristwatch and wallet, and stood crying by his body.

Because their counterparts on the Harlan County had been prevented from landing, 51 Canadian mounted police left Haiti. The United Nations evacuated most of its 200 human rights monitors to the Dominican Republic, and Prime Minister Malval acknowledged that his government had little left but moral authority.

The person in control of Haiti was Lt. Col. Michel Francois, police commander of Port-au-Prince, with thousands of paramilitary auxiliaries, known as *attachés*, at his disposal. They were given license to extort, rob or collect kickbacks from state agencies. Francois, himself, controlled the central bank, key port facilities, the only cement factory and the main rice mill.

President Clinton sent six naval warships to Haiti to help enforce the newly reimposed embargo and ordered an infantry company to Guantanamo Bay to protect, if necessary, the lives of about 1,000 Americans, including 140 U.S. Embassy personnel, living in Haiti. He also sent an additional 30 U.S. marines to guard the embassy. As the U.S. ships appeared on the horizon, Haitians fled to the countryside, fearing an invasion.

Republicans in Congress were extremely critical of Clinton's actions and called for re-examination of U.S. policy toward Haiti. Senate Minority Leader Robert Dole drafted an amendment to an appropriations bill to forbid the president to deploy U.S. military forces to Haiti without congressional authorization. He said that Clinton's policymakers had done a poor job and that "there's a lot of confusion, a lot of disarray." In a letter to Dole, Clinton wrote, "I am fundamentally opposed to amendments which would limit my abilities to perform my duties as commander-in-chief."

## *The Deadlock Continued*

The deadline for Cédras' resignation passed without any action on his part. In a letter to Dante Caputo, the UN special envoy to Haiti, Cédras wrote that the Governors Island Agreement "appears to be at a dead end" and challenged Caputo to a duel. There were reports from the provinces that many supporters of Aristide had been murdered and thrown into mass graves.

Aristide asked the U.S. government to protect members of his cabinet in Haiti and, if necessary, to give them sanctuary in the U.S. embassy. The United States responded by sending a fleet of armored automobiles for the use of Prime Minister Malval and members of his cabinet.

White House and U.S. Department of State officials held private meetings in Haiti with newly-arrived U.S. Ambassador William Swing, United Nations envoy Dante Caputo and Prime Minister Malval, designed to pave the way for Aristide's return on September 30, as called for in the Governors Island Agreement. One proposal called for Malval to make a speech of reconciliation and declare that he was prepared to expand his cabinet to include elements of Haiti's business and land-holding classes that had opposed Aristide's election and supported the military coup which had ousted him from power.

Aristide was not aware of these discussions. He learned of the proposed speech only after Malval, who did not like the idea, sent him a draft copy. Aristide agreed with Malval's objections and vetoed the speech. His supporters said it looked like a plot by the military to maintain a presence in any future Aristide government and to prevent Aristide from conducting much-needed reform on his return. In an interview on October 3, Malval rejected any expansion of his cabinet and said he would resign if Aristide was not restored to power by the end of the month, as called for by the Governors Island Agreement. The incident illustrated once more the lack of coordination among the main actors in the Haitian crisis.

## *Caught in a Vicious Circle*

Aristide's supporters began to despair and lose hope that he would ever return to Haiti. The police and military, using thousands of paramilitary auxiliares, had systematically destroyed community organizations. Resumption of the embargo left the poor with little more than rice to eat. Boat building for prospective refugees had ceased because no one had money to buy boats or for paying the sea passage. In any event, there was little hope for them getting through the multinational naval blockade. The entire structure of the brutal Tonton Macoutes was back in place.

A stalemate developed between Malval and the Army. Neither party was in a position to govern without support of the other. A senior aide to Malval commented, "We are in a situation that is very close to anarchy. We do not control the streets; the thugs control the streets." He stated, however, that Malval was not contemplating resigning because that would be equivalent to surrender.

Dante Caputo came up with a plan for the Haitian parliament to pass a broad amnesty law for civilian and military officers involved in the coup which ousted President Aristide, to be balanced by a bill which would separate the Haitian police from military control. But the idea did not progress. Pro-Aristide legislators controlled the Haitian Senate, but a pro-military faction controlled the lower chamber, the House of Delegates. In the final analysis, the bill collapsed because of failure to form a quorum in either chamber. Pro-Aristide legislators refused to attend because the police and military could not or would not guarantee their security. Since, under the Governors Island Agreement, an amnesty was a prerequisite to the resignation of Cédras and the return of Aristide, failure of parliament to act dealt a mortal blow to that agreement. The process was locked in a vicious circle. If the amnesty was not granted, Cédras would not resign. If Cédras did not resign, Aristide would not return. This, in effect, killed the Governors Island Agreement. Cédras had cleverly accomplished his goal of remaining in control in Haiti by assuring that parliament could not take the first step for him to leave — that of giving him an amnesty!

Anti-Aristide legislators accused pro-Aristide legislators of sabotaging the amnesty by failing to attend sessions, while friends of Aristide explained that most of their colleagues were in the United States afraid for their lives.

United Nations officials and assistants to Malval said a debate in the United States with respect to Aristide's mental health complicated the process. They said that U.S. Senator Jesse Helms called Aristide a "psychopath." This strengthened the army's belief that the United States really was not serious in wanting to restore him to office. One official stated that the debate had been "incredibly destructive and served to undermine everything we had worked for."

In a speech before the United Nations General Assembly Aristide asked for a total embargo against Haiti, by air and sea, to force the Haitian military to permit his return. But in Haiti, his prime minister, Robert Malval, remarked that "a total and complete blockade would be a heavy burden" for the country. Aristide further complicated his problems by calling for a seat for Taiwan in the United Nations. As a result, China blocked the UN Security Council from issuing a statement insisting on Aristide's return in compliance with the Governors Island Agreement. Only quick action by Haiti's delegation confirming Nationalist China's right to China's seat in that body, cleared the way for the Security Council resolution.

In Washington, the Clinton administration pressed the military regime in Haiti to make concessions but at the same time pressed pro-democracy legislators to accede to military demands. Clinton hinted that the United States was considering "other options" to pressure Haitian military leaders.

In Haiti, Emmanuel Constant, leader of FRAPH, the violent anti-Aristide group controlled by Police Chief Francois, called for elections within 90 days to form a new government to replace Aristide.

Needless to say, October 30, 1993 passed quietly without the restoration of Aristide to his legitimate position in Haiti.

In Washington, 44 prominent African Americans, including several members of congress, criticized President Clinton's strategy for ending military dictatorship in Haiti and urged him to consider multilateral action to restore President Aristide to his office in Haiti. However, the Clinton administration had decided not to undertake any new initiatives and chose instead to wait out the military government of Haiti as sanctions began to take effect.

But the sanctions had little effect on the military, except to increase their profits from smuggling, while they worsened the plight of poor farmers and villagers. The cumulative result was increasing malnutrition, deteriorating health care and, in some regions, hunger bordering on starvation. The military made it clear that it was they, not the international community, who would successfully wait out the embargo.

## *Gridlock Sets In*

It was clear that those working for the restoration of Aristide were in a weak position, casting about for solutions, sometimes at cross purposes. In Washington, Aristide's prime minister (Malval) called for a "gathering of salvation" where all sectors would express their views "to lay the groundwork for the implementation of the Governors Island accord" at the same time his minister of foreign affairs asked the United Nations to impose still tighter sanctions on the country in an effort to force the military leaders from power. Malval looked for indications that the United States had not lost its interest in Haiti but found little reassurance. The shadow of failure in Somalia had fallen over Haiti. After the loss of 18 American lives in an ambush in that country, President Clinton was reluctant to risk repeating the tragedy in Haiti.

U.S. officials urged Malval to broaden his cabinet to include political rivals of Aristide, a proposal Aristide rejected as an effort to weaken his authority. When Aristide learned that Malval's "gathering of salvation" was planned for Haiti and that the military would be invited to attend, Aristide refused to participate. Malval resigned in disgust.

It was revealed in *The New York Times* that Cédras and Francois had been paid as CIA informants for years.

*The Miami Herald* obtained a copy of a classified CIA memorandum, written by Brian Latell, its officer-in-charge of Latin America, after a visit to Haiti, in which Latell praised Cédras and stated that he had seen no evidence of oppressive rule in the country. At that time, Amnesty International estimated that more than 2,000 civilians had been killed by Haitian authorities since the 1991 coup. Its program director remarked, "That anyone could go to Haiti at that time and not observe repression by the military is absurd."

The desperation of the international community was reflected in a new effort by the "Four Friends of Haiti" at the United Nations (Canada, France, the United States and Venezuela) to persuade Cédras to comply with his 1993 commitment under the Governors Island Agreement to accept a military training mission to Haiti similar to the one which had sought to land from the Harlan County. As might have been expected, Cédras refused even to meet with their representatives.

As the year 1993 ended, armed members of the paramilitary organization FRAPH, with protection from uniformed Haitian military personnel, burned down over 200 homes of the poor in a night attack on the slum Cité Soleil in Port-au-Prince, an area inhabited principally by followers of President Aristide. Four persons lost their lives, five were wounded and an estimated 5,000 persons were left homeless. Most of the victims had been beaten and one was shot. Little was left to the slum except concrete foundations and rusty metal roofs. It was presumed that the attack was instigated to avenge the recent necklacing of the treasurer of FRAPH who lived nearby. From his exile in Washington, Aristide condemned "the reign of death and destruction" in his nation and called for help from the international community "to reinstate law and stability" in the country.

## *New Year, Old Problems*

After a burst of electrical power to celebrate New Year's Eve, the routine blackout of electricity resumed at 5 a.m. the following morning, reminding all residents of the beleaguered city of the disruptions of the UN-imposed embargo on their daily lives, while failing to achieve its aim of driving the military chiefs from power. It was becoming evident to many that only military action, or the very credible threat of impending military action, could remove them from power.

In a conversation with reporters, Aristide was asked about his feelings in this regard. His reaction was enthusiastic, but he reminded the reporters that his oath of office (Article 135-1 of the Haitian Constitution) required him to "maintain the nation's independence and the integrity of its territory." He could be impeached, he said, if he violated this oath.

In an interview with columnists and editorial writers, President Clinton made the unfortunate remark that Aristide's prospects for a return to Haiti had been "clouded" by his refusal of a plan by Prime Minister Malval for a national reconciliation conference. This remark led to speculation as to whether the President had abandoned his support for Aristide. Many White House denials were required to erase the impression that U.S. policy toward Haiti had changed.

It was obvious that ending the threat of a new wave of Haitian refugees headed for Florida was a principal motivation of U.S. policy toward Haiti. It was not surprising, therefore, that Aristide proposed a January conference in Miami on the theme, "Democracy: The Solution for the Refugee Crisis." It was obviously meant as a substitute for the reconciliation conference proposed for Haiti by his prime minister, but the theme was attractive from the point of view of both U.S. and United Nations policy toward Haiti.

## *The Miami Conference*

The Miami conference called by President Aristide took place over the weekend, January 14 through 16, 1994. It turned out to be pretty much a rally of Aristide supporters in which discussion of the refuge question was peripheral. It was not a working session in the sense of negotiations or attempts at reconciliation, since it was boycotted by both the Haitian military and the Haitian business community. Only two or three members of the parliamentary opposition to Aristide were present.

The U.S. Government was represented by the administration's point man on Haiti, Lawrence Pezzullo, and Michael Kozak, his assistant. Aristide was supported by his ambassador to Washington, Jean Casimir, and his minister of information and culture, Herve Denis. Several members of the U.S. Congress were present, including Representative Carrie P. Meek of Florida and Representative Major R. Owens, leader of the Congressional Task Force on Haiti.

Casimir said that the aim of the conference was not to arrive at new agreements with the military but rather to form a broad coalition of pro-democracy forces from Haiti and abroad, and to search for ways to place pressure on Haiti's military regime and its supporters.

Aristide played a marginal role. He opened the conference with a plea to the international community to restore democracy to Haiti and called for unity among his friends and for reaching out to his enemies. The representatives from the U.S. Department of State had feared he might use the meeting as a platform to criticize U.S. policy of forcibly returning Haitian refugees, but he did not.

Casimir recommended an even stronger embargo on Haiti. Pezzullo said existing sanctions would be reviewed, probably to curtail non-commercial air traffic in and out of Haiti, but said commercial flights and humanitarian shipments would not be affected. He promised that the United States would never relent on its policy of removing the military from power but that the Haitians, themselves, were responsible for building a consensus government. He said that steps could still be taken to implement the Governors Island Agreement and urged the Haitians to select a new prime minister and pass laws for an ultimate transfer of power from military to civilian rule.

Representative Meek said that military intervention in Haiti should be considered, and Representative Owens recommended training Haitian exiles for this purpose. Many Haitians at the conference were worried about tightening the embargo. They asserted it was making the poor miserable and the rich richer. Haitian senator Rony Mondestin commented, "You can not encourage democracy by strangling the country."

Perhaps the most significant recommendation to emerge was a call by Haitian legislators for Aristide to appoint a new prime minister and begin building a coalition government as soon as possible.

## The Embargo Reassessed

A small shipment of fuel, unloaded in Port-au-Prince to enable humanitarian organizations to distribute emergency aid to the poor and needy, reopened the debate on the effectiveness of the United Nations embargo on Haiti.

Supporters of the shipment — 300,000 gallons of diesel fuel and 100,000 gallons of gasoline — said it would reduce the suffering of the most vulnerable sectors of Haitian society without affecting the intended effect of the embargo on the military.

Those opposed to the shipment argued that the military would confiscate a large portion of the fuel and that the exception made by letting in this shipment would be widely interpreted as a collapse of the embargo.

There was no question that the embargo was having a devastating effect on the country, especially in the rural areas. Factories had shut down. Public transportation had come to a virtual standstill, and farmers were unable to ship their produce to market. The cost of basic foodstuffs rocketed, and the number of cases of severe malnutrition increased sharply. Hospitals lacked the facilities and supplies to save lives. Ambulances did not function, and families of patients had to provide them with food. The principal source of cash came from the sale of charcoal, made by cutting trees from the hillsides. People were actually cutting down their own fruit trees for this purpose and were eating seeds meant for future planting. For the first time since records were kept, beginning in 1988, famine levels were reached in many communities. Health officials estimated that at least 10,000 persons had died as a direct or indirect result of the sanctions. Much humanitarian aid was being sold on the black market.

In the meantime, the four so-called "Friends of Haiti," the United States, France, Canada and Venezuela, prepared to ask the United Nations for a near total embargo on trade to Haiti, except for food and humanitarian supplies.

For the first time, the international community considered targeting sanctions to individuals or groups. One proposed measure would have prohibited non-scheduled flights to and from Haiti in order to end the practice of military officers and their civilian backers sending planes to such destinations as Miami and Mexico for the purpose of stocking up on luxury items and embargoed goods. The same measure would have provided legal basis for governments to block bank accounts and other assets maintained by Haitian military officers outside Haiti. The United States had already blocked the assets of 41 Haitians involved in the coup against Aristide. The U.S. Treasury Department announced the addition of 523 Haitian military officers to the list, virtually the entire officer corps and their families, and the U.S. State Department revoked the visas for travel to the United States of all Haitian officers.

One problem with the embargo was impossible to overcome — the smuggling of petroleum products from the Dominican Republic by land and water. Gasoline imported into the Dominican Republic at a dollar a gallon could be sold in Haiti for up to $10 a gallon. Because of the immense profits that could be made through contraband trade, it was impossible to prevent the entry into Haiti of fuel and gasoline from its neighbor to the east. It was estimated that half the army of the Dominican Republic was distributed along the border, presumably to prevent smuggling, but many soldiers accepted bribes to look the other way or succumbed to the temptation of benefiting themselves from the illegal trade.

In the meantime it was announced that U.S. trade with Haiti had increased almost 50% over the previous year as a result of a U.S. exemption to the embargo which permitted, for "humanitarian reasons of preserving the jobs of Haitian workers," importation into the United States of goods assembled in Haiti from materials imported from the United States.

Also, the U.S. Embassy and other diplomatic missions in Haiti violated the embargo by routinely buying smuggled fuel on the black market, claiming it was the only way they could continue to carry out their business.

# Chapter VIII

# Haitian Policy in Crisis

In the early months of 1994, disagreement broke out between President Aristide and the Clinton administration over steps to be taken to solve the Haitian crisis and restore him to his legitimate position in Haiti.

A United States plan, backed by the United Nations, called on Aristide to name a new prime minister and create a government of national unity which would press the Haitian parliament to enact an amnesty law to induce the military leaders of Haiti to resign from their positions. If they did, the prime minister and Aristide would negotiate terms for his return, but no date was set for his return.

Aristide's position was that Cédras and Francois should first step down, as called for in the Governors Island Agreement. Haiti's parliament would then adopt a general amnesty law and measures to reform the police and armed forces. The United Nations would then resume the technical assistance program it was forced to abandon in 1993. Only after these steps were completed would he name a prime minister and return to Haiti. United Nations sanctions on Haiti would be lifted only after he resumed the presidency in Haiti.

Aristide rebuked the international community for what he called "delaying tactics" and complicity. If the international community really wanted to restore democracy in Haiti, he said, it would have done so long ago. "There are promises." he asserted, "but there is still no clearcut, firm expression of political will."

Fortunately for Aristide, the US/UN plan was torpedoed by the military leaders of Haiti and their allies in the Haitian parliament.

## *Aristide Terminates U.S. Treaty*

On another front, Aristide sent President Clinton a letter informing him that he was giving the United States six months notice of his intention to abrogate a 1981 treaty with the United States which gave U.S. officials the right to board Haitian vessels to search for illegal immigrants and return them to Haiti. Aristide said he was renouncing the agreement because the United States had violated its obligation to provide refuge for Haitians fleeing persecution and was exposing repatriated refugees to mortal danger.

President Clinton refused to abandon his policy of forceful repatriation, but Aristide's threat had the effect of triggering a new round of serious discussions at the highest levels of the U.S. government on how to end the military dictatorship in Haiti and restore Aristide to his rightful position as head of government in that country.

Two weeks later, at a press conference, Aristide called Clinton's long-standing order to repatriate Haitian refugees "a cynical joke" and a "racist policy" that had turned Haiti into a concentration camp where the military can terrorize and murder the people at will.

"Every day," he said, "people are murdered and pigs are eating their corpses. How many murders does it take to create a holocaust?"

His words did not sit well with the White House but they were confirmed by reports from Haiti which described a new wave of military terrorism in the country which left hundreds of dead and thousands in hiding. This action, carried out by FRAPH and the *attachés*, included the rape of women, kidnapping of small children of pro-Aristide activists, the mutilation of bodies, and dumping them in public places. The terror was directed toward maintaining the supremacy of the army and destroying all vestiges of Aristide support.

## *Aristide's U.S. Supporters Act*

On March 23, 1994, a nearly full-page illustrated advertisement addressed to President Clinton appeared in *The New York Times*. It contained the text of a blunt 248-word letter denouncing his policies on Haiti and carried the names of an inter-racial group of 95 prominent liberals, among them Hollywood actors and artists and civil rights, union, religious and political leaders, including members of the Congressional Black Caucus. Most of them had been close friends and supporters of the president in the past.

The letter read as follows:

Dear Mr. President:
Guy Malary, Haiti's Minister of Justice, was killed by assassins linked to the Haitian military in broad daylight on October 14, 1993. Mr. Malary, an internationally respected American-trained lawyer, had accepted his post with a reluctance counterbalanced by his reverence for democracy and the rule of law. For principles all Americans cherish, he gave his life.

While Mr. Malary may be the most widely known victim of Haiti's tyrannical military regime, over three thousand more ordinary Haitians have paid a price no less dear. Still others continue to flee their island, desperately heading for safer shores. International law and precepts of common decency require our nation to provide fleeing Haitian political refugees safe haven until democracy can be restored in their country. Surely we cannot as a society justify treating Haitians any differently than the thousand of Cubans, Vietnamese, Eastern Europeans and others we have shielded over the years.

Mr. President, we do not suggest that our nation has an unbounded capacity to absorb refugees. We do however urge that the process pursuant to which we grant safe haven to refugees be colorblind. The United States has effectively sealed Haitian political refugees into the death chamber of their own island. In no other case, against no other people has our nation employed measures of automatic repatriation. Why just the Haitians? One is left to reasonably conclude that our policy is driven by considerations of race. No other explanation of this untenable distinction seems plausible.

Sincerely,

Ninety-five names with identifications followed.

In addition, the advertisement carried a coupon which the reader could clip for sending a tax-deductible contribution to TransAfrica in Washington, D.C., an organization known for its world-wide promotion of black causes, notably the Free South Africa Movement.

The same issue of the *Times* carried strong criticism of Clinton's Haitian policy in a long column written by Bob Hebert. And the same day that the *Times* ad appeared, *The Washington Post* carried a letter to the editor by one of the signers of the *Times* ad, Corrine Brown, Democratic Representative from Florida. It was a scorching criticism of Robert D. Novak, a *Post* columnist, who had written several articles in support of Haiti's military leaders and their brutal organization, FRAPH.

Most critics accused the Clinton administration of undermining Aristide and supporting a dubious plan for returning him to Haiti. They asked for more forceful leadership to remove the military from power, even the use of U.S. and foreign troops. Democratic Representative Major R. Owens of New York, leader of the 40-member Congressional Black Caucus, asserted, "we are upset; we are indignant; and we are declaring war on a racist policy." He said the "war" would involve mobilizing churches and civil disobedience, including a national day of protest at federal facilities. The caucus listed eleven measures the administration should take, among them

1. Expand the commercial and trade embargo on Haiti, except for food and medicine;
2. Sever all air links to Haiti;
3. Deny visas to Haitian military leaders and freeze their assets;
4. Press for deployment of a multinational border patrol between Haiti and the Dominican Republic to prevent violation of existing sanctions on Haiti;
5. Stop the interdiction and summary repatriation of Haitian refugees.

Caucus members also called for the resignation of Lawrence A. Pezzullo, the administration's special envoy to Haiti.

The public and congressional pressure on Clinton was effective. He reversed the administration's policy, promising to wring concessions from the Haitian military rather than from Aristide. The new policy, he said, would be designed to bring U.S. positions closer to those of Aristide, rather than requiring him to make wholesale concessions to his enemies.

The Clinton administration crafted a new plan for restoring Aristide. Three key steps would occur on the same day: The military would step down; Haiti's parliament would confirm a new prime minister named by Aristide; and a law granting amnesty to the military leaders would be enacted. Unless Haiti's military agreed to the new plan, the United States would press the UN Security Council to approve a tougher and mandatory embargo on Haiti to include all items except food and medicine, to replace the voluntary one then in place.

The administration also pledged to try to compel the Dominican Republic to increase its efforts to block widespread smuggling of fuel across its border with Haiti.

# Pressure on Clinton Mounts

Despite President Clinton's determination to improve U.S. policy toward Haiti, little progress was made and domestic criticism intensified. Deadlock continued among the principal actors involved, between President Aristide and the military on the one hand and The White House and members of Congress on the other. The military leaders in Haiti appeared entrenched in their positions as the trade embargo failed to dislodge them from power. The policies of the Clinton administration had reached a stalemate and despair and pessimism set in. A growing number of people believed that Aristide might never be restored to power. A team of administration officials, led by Lawrence A. Pezzullo, U.S. special envoy to Haiti, sought to defend U.S. policy toward Haiti in hearings before the Senate Foreign Relations sub-committee on Western Hemisphere Affairs. Pezzullo reiterated the U.S. position that a broad-based government had to be in place in Haiti, ready to fill the vacuum if the army should surrender the power it seized in the 1991 coup. Aristide had already rejected pressure to form such a government because a provisional agreement failed to set a date for his return and he feared that his political foes would use such an agreement to dilute his political power in Haiti.

Pezzullo blamed Aristide for the impasse. He and the other officials who testified, Walter Slocumbe, deputy secretary of defense, and Mark L. Schneider, assistant administer at the Agency for International Development, sought to defend the administration's position despite a daylong barrage of criticism from Democratic members of Congress and private humanitarian organizations who served as witnesses.

Some of the critics, including Representative Joseph P. Kennedy II (D-Mass.) called for the threat of military intervention to make the Haitian military "recognize that the United States was willing to put its troops on the line." The possibility of such action was immediately dismissed by Slocumbe, who stated that the United States had no desire to use military force in Haiti and no plans to do so. (Without doubt this was good news to Cédras and company in Haiti.) The possibility of joint U.S.-UN-OAS action was not discussed.

Two prominent human rights organizations, Human Rights/America and the National Coalition for Haitian Refugees, issued a joint report charging that Clinton's policy toward Haiti had given the military rulers of Haiti a green light to continue massive human rights abuses without fear of punishment. The two organizations stated in their report that

"President Clinton's policy of disregarding fundamental human rights issues to resolve Haiti's political crisis, combined with his inhumane and illegal practice of summarily returning Haitian refugees, has contributed to a human rights disaster that has tarnished his presidency and discredited its stated commitment to democracy and human rights around the world." They accused Lawrence Pezzullo of making "constant concessions" to the military.

Their report concluded that U.S. policy should be scrapped and replaced by an approach that would hold the Haitian armed forces responsible for rights abuses, end the summary repatriation of Haitian boat people and marshal a concerted, international campaign through the United Nations and the Organization of American States to exert new pressures that the military would not be able to ignore. They urged that Pezzullo be replaced.

The report's language was the harshest to date in the rising chorus of criticism that had been directed against the Clinton administration for its failure to make good on its promise to restore Haitian democracy and return Aristide to office.

Influential columnists were also relentless in their criticism. In the widely read *Washington Post*, Richard Cohen wrote, "If there is a worse foreign policy botch than Haiti, nothing comes to mind. The policy is a debacle and almost totally discredited." He deplored the difference in treatment of Haitian refugees from those of Cuba. If conditions in Haiti persist, he said, Washington has to be prepared to use some muscle."

In two articles in the *Post*, one of its most respected columnists, Mary McGrory, wrote that Haiti offered Clinton the opportunity to show the world that the United States keeps its promises. "Resolution of the Haitian problem." she said, "now requires the use of force."

Clarence Page, a nationally syndicated columnist, observed, "I find Clinton on the subject of race to be uplifting, yet perplexing. He knows human nature well enough to sing the right words and music. Yet when his feet hit the floor on thorny issues like Haiti, they seem to dance out of step."

In *Time* magazine, Cathy Booth wrote a long pessimistic report on Haiti describing the ineffectiveness of the United Nations embargo, the effects on Haiti of Clinton's shifting policies, the campaign of terror waged by paramilitary groups against Aristide supporters, and the cleaning of the streets of Haiti at an annual cost of $2 million dollars to the U.S. taxpayers, among other kindred subjects.

In a severe critique of U.S. Haitian policy in an editorial April 25, 1994, *The Washington Post* concluded that U.S. indecision in its Haitian policy was intolerable. "The crimes being committed . . . make it necessary to consider the possibility of an international force capable of sweeping up the most guilty." *The Post* suggested bringing in "the contingent of French-speaking police advisers and training officers that was ready to go last summer. . . . This country (the United States) has a humanitarian duty to end the mayhem that Haitian soldiers are inflicting upon the Haitian people. . . . The present policy under which American ships keep Haitians penned up on their island, while armed thugs hunt down their adversaries, violates fundamental American principles."

In recommending consideration of international military action, *The Washington Post* returned full circle to its editorial position of October 2, 1991, two days after Aristide was overthrown, when it suggested an international peace force to return President Aristide to office.

Members of Congress became involved. David R. Obey (D-Wis.), Chairman of the House Appropriations Committee, called for a military invasion of Haiti to remove the country's military commanders in order to clear the way for Aristide's return. He said it was preferable to use an international force, but if that was not possible, U.S. troops should enter the country on their own.

Under Obey's proposal, an international or U.S. force would remove the Haitian military commanders and then be replaced by a Latin American security force operating under U.N. auspices.

On April 19, 1994 five liberal Democratic senators — Tom Harkin of Iowa, Christopher Dodd of Connecticut, Carol Mosely-Braun of Illinois, Paul Wellstone of Minnesota and Richard Feingold of Wisconsin — introduced legislation to impose new sanctions against Haiti's military leaders.

"President Clinton is a good man and a decent human being, but his policy toward Haiti is unconscionable," Harkin said. "It is bankrupt, morally and politically, and we have to change it." Failure to stand up to "thuggery" in Haiti, the group said, seemed certain to damage U.S. credibility throughout the world.

"If we can't stand up for democracy and human rights in our hemisphere, then what do the Serbs have to fear?" Harkin asked. "If we can't do it in our own hemisphere, how can we stand strong a half a world away?"

The proposed legislation would have imposed a complete ban on commercial trade with Haiti, cut off air links with the United States, denied visas to members of the Haitian armed forces and their civilian supporters and frozen any assets they had in the United States. The bill would also have changed U.S. refugee policy by barring funds for the return of any boat people who were denied a proper hearing of their claims for political asylum in the United States. In addition, it would have cut off U.S. aid to any country that refused to cooperate with the embargo.

Three days later six members of the U.S. House of Representatives were arrested on civil disobedience charges while protesting U.S. policy toward Haiti in front of the White House, especially the president's policy of returning black refugees to Haiti while refugees from other countries were given political asylum.

The group was composed of five members of the Congressional Black Caucus, its Chairman Kweisi Mfume (D-MD), Donald Payne (D-NJ), Barbara-Rose Collins (D-MI), Ronald Dellums (D-CA) and Major Owens (D-NY) plus Joseph P. Kennedy II (D-MA).

Although the group had obtained a permit to demonstrate, U.S. Park Policeman Lt. Dennis Hayo revoked it when the six, surrounded by tourists and journalists, illegally halted in front of the North Portico. As called for by government regulations, Lt. Hayo warned them three times to disband or face arrest. After kneeling for a moment on the sidewalk, each was bound by Flexicuffs, had their belongings confiscated, had their photographs taken with an arresting officer, and were loaded into a police wagon.

The six were charged with demonstrating without a permit and were released with citations to appear for a hearing. Under the U.S. Constitution, members of congress are immune from arrest, but none of the protestors claimed that immunity. Indeed, they had sought arrest in order to call attention to what they considered unjust policies toward Haiti. Mfume asserted that the demonstration was only the first that would be made before government buildings. Kennedy said it was time for Americans to reassert moral leadership on Haiti.

## *The Robinson Hunger Strike*

An important part of such protests was a 27-day hunger strike by Randall Robinson, executive director of the lobby group, TransAfrica.

Robinson gained fame and respect in the 1980s when he organized the Free South Africa Movement to help end apartheid in South Africa. His hunger strike for Haiti began on April 12, 1994. It was in protest against President Clinton's policy of forceful repatriation of Haitian refugees without giving them opportunity for a hearing on their possible claims for political asylum. Robinson also called for stiffer sanctions against Haitian military leaders.

The strike took place in the basement of TransAfrica headquarters in Washington, D.C. It was not an act of bravado or showmanship. It was the result of a moral commitment on his part. He vowed to continue his fast until death if necessary, or until public opinion forced the president to relent on what he considered to be a profoundly racist and immoral policy. At 52 years of age, a lanky 6'5 in height and normally weighing 200 pounds, he had no need to lose weight but felt he had a moral obligation to do what he could to call attention to the need for change in the policy of the United States toward the island republic.

During his hunger strike, Robinson drank only juice and water. His health was monitored on a daily basis by a medical doctor. After two weeks, he became dehydrated and lost eight pounds. The protein level in his blood dropped below normal. But he said he was not afraid to die. "Hundreds of people have died because of Bill Clinton," he said. "My risk is small compared to theirs."

He was frequently visited by reporters and he held a joint press conference with President Aristide. As a result, his efforts received considerable media coverage, and editorial support of his cause was broad.

His fast also began to generate results. George Withers, press secretary of the U.S. House Armed Services Committee, said that, as a result of Robinson's strike, a number of members of Congress had signed on as co-sponsors of a Congressional Black Caucus bill on Haiti. Also, each Friday a group of about 50 persons gathered in a vigil at the TransAfrica building. As Robinson became weaker public and media protests against the administration's Haiti policy became stronger.

One reporter, Laura Blumenfeld, traced Robinson's condition on a daily basis for *The Washington Post*. Day 18 was particularly difficult, she wrote. Robinson had not slept. His weight had dropped 12 pounds, and his body temperature had fallen. On Day 20 he was visited by Samuel Berger, White House deputy national security advisor, and Morton Halperin, special assistant to the president for national security.

They sought, without success, to persuade Robinson of the validity of Clinton's refugee policy. Robinson said he only wanted Clinton to keep his campaign pledge to end former President Bush's policy of forceful repatriation. Halperin commented on leaving that Robinson seemed "committed, sincere and dedicated."

By Day 21, Robinson was confined to bed, spoke with a stutter, and gestured only with his fingers. Blumenfeld sensed despair in his demeanor. She quoted Robinson as saying "I have no sense of whether I will succeed."

Day 22 brought the good news that 86 intercepted Haitian refugees had been taken to a detention center near Miami, where they would be held until their claims for asylum could be reviewed. Robinson restrained any desire to celebrate. "This is just one boat," he said, implying that until he was sure that Clinton had permanently altered U.S. refugee policy, the black banner outside his headquarters would continue to fly and he would continue to fast.

On May 4, 1994, William Raspberry wrote in *The Washington Post*, "I think it (Clinton's Haitian refugee policy) is changing, Since Robinson's strike, two groups of Haitians have been intercepted by the Coast Guard — some 400 on April 22 and another 97 yesterday. Both, according to the administration, involved 'unique' situations. But both groups were taken to U.S. shores.

"If that's the right thing to do," he continued, "why not announce it? It's the right thing to do and it would save the life of a good man."

Amnesty International reported that since the beginning of 1994, 139 of 904 Haitians forcibly returned to Haiti had been arrested and others ill-treated. Many persons who tried to make asylum claims in Haiti had to wait months for an interview and many had to remain in hiding or face persecution.

On Day 23 of his hunger strike, Robinson's metabolism had just about ground to a halt and his body had started to feed on its own fat and muscle, including the heart muscle. He was hospitalized for dehydration and fed intravenously. His physician had recommended hospitalization after his heartbeat increased to 112 beats a minute. He became so weak that his blood pressure was unstable. Being in a hospital, however, his life was no longer in danger, His doctor did not advise him to end his hunger strike, but remained alert for danger signs.

Clinton finally got around to saying, "I understand and respect what he's doing, and we ought to change our policy." Whereupon Clinton said that the United States would set up new refugee processing centers aboard U.S. ships, or U.S.-contracted ships, or in third countries, as well as new U.S. processing centers inside Haiti.

This seemed to satisfy Robinson. On the 27th day of his hunger strike he applauded Clinton for his new refugee policy and ended his fast.

## *Pezzullo Dismissed*

On April 27, 1994, in what was generally interpreted as admission of a failing policy toward Haiti, the U.S. Department of State announced the resignation of Lawrence A. Pezzullo, special U.S. envoy to Haiti, effective April 29, 1994.

Pezzullo, former U.S. ambassador to Nicaragua, who had previously served as head of Catholic Relief Services and had been appointed by President Clinton in March 1993, helped negotiate the Governors Island Agreement of July 1993 between President Aristide and Lt. Gen. Raoul Cédras, commander-in-chief of the Haitian armed forces. When Cédras failed to honor that agreement, Pezzullo sought other means to resolve the Haitian crisis. One of these was to try to persuade Aristide to make concessions to his opponents in Haiti, a policy which Aristide found insulting, since he was the one who had been deprived of his legitimate rights. The pressure placed on Aristide in this regard was a factor in Aristide's quarrel with President Clinton. Supporters of Aristide considered Pezzullo responsible for failed U.S. policy toward Haiti and had clamored for his resignation.

# Chapter IX
# Tightening the Screws

Stung by the public criticism of his policy toward Haiti, President Clinton on April 28, 1994 recast that policy to reflect a tougher stance toward that nation's military leaders and a more cooperative position toward President Aristide. Its main aims would be:

1.  To ask the UN Security Council to impose a global trade embargo on Haiti, plus financial sanctions and a travel ban against about 600 military officers who supported the regime or participated in the coup against President Aristide.
2.  To demand the resignation of army chief of staff Lt. Gen. Raoul Cédras, his deputy, Brigadier Gen. Phillippe Biamby, and Port-au-Prince Police Chief, Lt. Col. Michel Francois. They would be given 15 days to resign and would be encouraged to leave the country prior to imposition of the trade embargo.
3.  After these leaders had left their posts, to ask Aristide to name a new prime minister and to take other steps called for in the 1993 Governors Island Agreement.
4.  To press the Dominican Republic to enforce sanctions along its border with Haiti, and
5.  To seek to increase the number of UN human rights observers in Haiti from 50 to 260, the size of the contingent before the Governors Island accord collapsed.

In Haiti diplomats, relief workers and supporters of Aristide believed that sanctions against the military would come too late to be effective unless they were backed by a credible threat of the use of force. Analysts said that if such a threat did not exist, the military officers who ruled the country would remain in control while the suffering of the poor intensified.

Rev. Antoine Adrien, Roman Catholic priest and adviser to Aristide, said, "the Clinton administration has lost credibility not only with the Haitian people but also with the military. They no longer think that the Clinton administration is serious about anything they say or do."

Diplomats felt that the army had networks and structures in place to circumvent the embargo, even to profit from it. The new oil sanctions would have minimal effect, since they came at a time when the output of electrical energy in the country was at its peak. The Peligre hydroelectric dam, which provided 40% of the electricity of Port-au-Prince, had been repaired and, following heavy rains, had greatly increased its production, reducing the number of blackouts in the city. Also, much equipment requiring electrical energy had been converted to burn propane gas. As fuel used for cooking, it was exempted from the embargo.

One Haitian analyst said, "you either escalate or you pull out. The mistake has been to think you can have diplomacy without the threat of force, when the only syntax the army understands is force. Now the misery index will certainly go up, but there is no certainty of achieving the political results."

A sign of growing confidence in military ranks was a bill in the Haitian parliament to declare the presidency vacant and to name Emile Jonaissant, head of the Supreme Court, acting president of Haiti. The bill would also have provided for new elections in December.

Once again The White House considered dispatching military trainers to Haiti along the lines of the aborted Harlan County mission of October 1993. Lawrence Pezzullo, who, after his forced resignation April 29, became a severe critic of administration policy on Haiti, laughed when he learned that the idea of a training mission was being revived. He said that when he argued in 1993 that the troops on the Harlan County should land, even in the face of Haitian protests, Secretary of State Warren Christopher had declined to support his proposal.

The idea was dropped then and again in 1994. But Clinton said for the first time that he would not rule out the use of force to oust the military from power. Various military options were discussed but none were agreed upon. Instead, Clinton's 5-point policy plan was strengthened to include four new aims:

1. To eliminate exemptions under the embargo for assembly industries.
2. To close the Haitian-Dominican border entirely.
3. To help retrain the Haitian military at some future time, and
4. To increase the number of Haitians receiving food aid from 900,000 to 1.2 million.

## The UN Takes Action

On May 6, 1994, in response to a petition by the United States, and under authority of the UN Charter, the UN Security Council, by unanimous vote, approved a near-total trade embargo on Haiti, as well as financial and travel restrictions on Haiti's military leaders. They were to go into effect until May 21, thereby providing 15 days for Haiti's three top military leaders to resign and spare their nation this disaster. They were specifically named in the resolution. Only medicine, food and cooking oil were exempted from the embargo, and the sanctions were to be imposed immediately.

The travel restrictions banned all flights by private planes to and from Haiti. Their purpose was to preclude wealthy Haitians and all military and police officers and their most prominent civilian supporters from using their own aircraft to circumvent the embargo. The Security Council also urged a worldwide freeze on the assets of coup leaders and their supporters. President Balaguer of the Dominican Republic asked the United Nations to station monitors along his nation's border with Haiti. The Security Council agreed not to lift the sanctions until the military leaders in Haiti were gone, the police and military commands had been reformed, the legislature had adopted a political amnesty and Aristide was back in office.

In a separate report, UN Secretary General Boutros Boutros-Ghali warned the international community that in the past it had taken on a "prejudicial role" which had encouraged Haitians to take refuge rather than working among themselves for a settlement. He warned that international efforts would fail without a willingness to compromise on all sides. He also accused the Haitian military at waging an intensive campaign of repression against Aristide's followers in Haiti, including at least a dozen cases of politically-motivated rape. The number of murders remained at an alarming level, he wrote, and there were large numbers of arbitrary arrests, illegal detentions, abductions and enforced disappearances, as well as secret detention centers in Port-au-Prince.

U.S. officials said that aid agencies, which were already helping to feed a million Haitians a day, would add an additional 400,000 to try to counter the effect of the trade embargo on the poor. But they said that the United States would not consider sending U.S. soldiers to train the Haitian military and police until safe conditions for their work existed.

## Congress Divided on U.S. Role

A growing number of liberal Democrats in the U.S. Congress became convinced that the only way to dislodge the Haitian military leaders from power was to use force. Other lawmakers, mostly moderates and conservatives, were strongly opposed to such action, saying that military intervention would lead to a long period of occupation and would not accomplish the goal of converting Haiti to a democracy. Still others were willing to wait out the new UN embargo and sanctions, hoping that these would bring the Haitian commanders to their knees.

House Speaker Tom Foley said that he, too, was willing to consider military force as an option but stressed that Congress should be thoroughly consulted beforehand. The principal question, he said, would be the exit strategy once the United States became involved.

There was doubt that either chamber would approve a U.S. intervention. In the Senate, Majority Leader George Mitchell and Minority Leader Robert Dole were strongly opposed. Dole called for a bipartisan fact-finding commission to take "a fresh look at the situation in Haiti." The idea was immediately endorsed by General Cédras in Haiti. Everyone was interested in debating the pros and cons of a unilateral U.S. invasion. No one, it seemed, gave thought to the possibility of UN-authorized multilateral military intervention.

Some Congressmen felt that quick, decisive military action by U.S. armed forces would not require congressional approval. Senator Bob Graham of Florida said that Clinton should first explain to the American people why such action was required. He reminded that neither President Bush's invasion of Panama nor President Reagan's invasion of Grenada was given prior approval by Congress.

Representative Alcee Hastings of Florida said, "We should stabilize Haiti or we'll have to stabilize Haitians in Miami." Senator Christopher J. Dodd and House Armed Forces Committee Chairman Ronald V. Dellums called on a ban on all commercial flights to Haiti and mandatory sanctions on third countries that violated the embargo.

On May 8, 1994, as relations with Congress became more delicate, President Clinton appointed William H. Gray III, former Pennsylvania congressman, to be his new special envoy to Haiti. He replaced Lawrence Pezzullo who was forced to resign from this position the previous week, leaving the U.S. Department of State rudderless on Haitian policy at the working level. Gray said he was taking the position as a private citizen without pay as a special employee for a maximum of 130 days. He was expected to better relations with Congress and develop more forceful policies than his predecessor, in keeping with Clinton's new policy of tightening the screws on the Haitian military. It seemed a formidable task for anyone to accomplish in little more than four months.

## The Refugee Problem Returns

One of the most urgent problems that Gray faced was how to handle the resurgent problem of dealing with the increased number of Haitian boat people fleeing their country and seeking to reach the shores of Florida. On the one hand Clinton had denounced Haiti's military dictators as blood-stained tyrants; on the other hand, he insisted on returning the vast majority of fleeing Haitians to the possibility of further persecution by these very same tyrants.

Part of the problem stemmed from the fact that the United States had no fixed method for processing refugees. At different times Haitian refugees had been processed in Florida, aboard Coast Guard cutters, at Guantanamo Bay Naval Base in Cuba, and in Haiti itself. Where refugees were processed, how they were processed and the criteria used in the processing were key factors affecting the decision as to who would be given asylum and who would be returned to Haiti, and these factors could vary considerably from time to time and place to place. For example, refugees had a better chance of asylum if processed on land than on board a vessel. The facilities aboard ship were usually inadequate for the job, from the standpoint of lack of trained interviewers and, from the point of view of applicants, support groups to help them present their cases. Applicants had the best chance of acceptance if processed at centers within Haiti, but were more exposed to reprisals from the military and police and their auxiliary forces who hovered around these centers seeking dissidents. At different times acceptance rates varied from six to 19 percent, depending upon sites and criteria used for interviews.

A perennial problem was what to do with refugees who had AIDS or tested positively for the AIDS virus. Even if they were eligible for asylum, placement of these unfortunate persons — in families, in hospitals or with charitable organizations — was difficult. Another complicating factor, rarely mentioned publicly but underlining many decisions with respect to the acceptance of refugees by the United States, was anti-refugee sentiment, especially in Florida, a State inundated with both Cuban and Haitian refugees and with one of the largest numbers of electoral votes in U.S. presidential elections. This accounted for President Bush's hardline policy toward Haitian refugees in 1992, a presidential election year, and was a factor in President Clinton's decision to continue this same policy of forced repatriation. With mid-term elections scheduled for November 8, 1994 and his own re-election campaign for the presidency scheduled to begin in 1995, President Clinton did not want to antagonize the voters of Florida. In fact, Florida Governor Lawton Chiles had already filed a suit against the federal government to recoup the millions of dollars he had to spend for caring for, teaching and incarcerating illegal immigrants.

On the other hand Clinton was being pressured by advocacy groups, many of which had political clout, for example, the Congressional Black Caucus and the National Association for the Advancement of Colored People. Some of these groups recommended the establishment of refugee camps or temporary safe havens for Haitians in other countries, and Clinton indicated a desire to involve other nations and international organizations in sharing the burden.

Soon after, the United Nations High Commissioner for Refugees, Mrs. Sadako Ogata, agreed to participate in the processing and settlement of Haitian boat people seeking entry into the United States and other countries. Her involvement was important to the United States because it lent international credibility to U.S. refugee policies. The High Commissioner would be involved more in policy and diplomatic contacts than in actual operations but this in itself helped convince other governments that the Haitians refugee crisis was an international issue and not merely a bilateral quarrel between Haiti and the United States.

## *A Nation Divided*

During this period both the U.S. Government and U.S. public opinion were divided on whether the United States should invade Haiti to oust that nation's murderous military dictatorship and restore Jean-Bertrand

Aristide to his rightful position as the freely-elected president of that country.

Investigative reporters Rowland Evans and Robert Novak scored a journalistic scoop in reporting on an unannounced meeting on Haiti at the White House on May 7, 1994 between President Clinton and General John Shalikashvili, chairman of the U.S. Joint Chiefs of Staff.

The most revealing parts of their article, published in *The Washington Post* on May 19, 1994, was as follows:

> Clinton surprised the chairman of the Joint Chiefs by revealing his "reluctant" feeling that only an invasion could restore exiled Haitian President Jean-Bertrand Aristide to power.

> The president wanted to see military options and even proposed a tentative D-Day: mid-May . . . Shalikashvili had no trouble laying out the negatives. . . . At that meeting . . . invasion plans were put on hold.

Four days later an event in Haiti gave Clinton cause for further reflection. On May 11, 1994, in a defiant move by the Haitian military, the pro-military head of Haiti's supreme court, Judge Emile Jonaissant, 81, was installed as provisional president of Haiti in place of absent president Jean-Bertrand Aristide. It was interpreted as a gesture directed against the intensified efforts of the United States to force the military to step down and allow Aristide to return to power. It strongly implied that the military had no intention of submitting to U.S. and UN demands. Jonaissant was given the immediate responsibility of naming a new prime minister and cabinet and organizing elections so that a new president could take office on February 7, 1995. Cédras indicated an interest in campaigning for the post.

Diplomats and Western observers in Haiti said that Jonaissant's appointment was unconstitutional, since it was made by the Senate alone, without approval of the Chamber of Deputies, as called for by the constitution. The Clinton administration called the installation illegal. White House spokesperson Dee Dee Myers said, "We don't recognize that there is a vacancy in the office of President." Strobe Talbott, Deputy Secretary of State, said, "This is a blatant attempt by an illegal faction of the Haitian Senate, with the assistance of the military, to install a bogus de facto government."

In Haiti caretaker prime minister Robert Malval ordered all state workers to ignore any orders from Jonaissant or Cédras. He accused

Cédras of cowardice and treason and demanded that he resign. A few hours later Jonaissant issued a decree stating that he would serve as both provisional president and premier, violating a provision of the Haitian constitution separating these two positions. The decree also listed his cabinet selections.

Clearly Cédras was not making plans to step down from power. He was cleverly constructing a new governmental structure completely under his command. He was even in a position to arrange for his own election as next president of Haiti, thereby shutting off Aristide, perhaps forever.

The case for invading Haiti was convincingly laid out in *The Washington Post* of May 13, 1994 in an article by Richard Haass, formerly a senior member of the National Security Council staff in the Bush administration, and Stephen Solarz, former Democratic congressman from New York. Pertinent excerpts follow:

> U.S. policy (toward Haiti) is not working. As a consequence, both Haitian democracy and American credibility are on the line. . . .

> Further diplomatic efforts to broker a deal by which the current military leaders would step down and President Aristide would return are almost certain to fail. . . . Yet, without the return of Aristide . . . it is impossible to conceive of a settlement that would result in the reestablishment of a legitimate democratic government in Port-au-Prince. . . .

> A military intervention need not and should not be undertaken by the United States alone. . . . There is an alternative: multilateral intervention. A U.S.-led coalition could include forces from Canada, Venezuela, France and the Caribbean. Such an approach might receive UN . . . support. . . .

> Defeating the small, lightly armed and poorly trained Haitian military would not be hard. If Desert Storm took six weeks, "Caribbean Hurricane" would take six hours.

> The real challenge would come not in winning the "war" but in securing the peace. In such situations, getting in is always easier than getting out. Yet an exit strategy is entirely feasible. The United States could take on the lion's share of the initial operation. But most of the manpower for the subsequent task of providing security and establishing a reliable indigenous force capable of maintaining law and order throughout Haiti could come from the other countries in the coalition.

Someone in The White House must have taken careful note of the Haass-Solarz recommendations. With minor adjustments, they were successfully applied to Haiti five months later (see Chapter X).

Randall Robinson came back into the limelight with an article in *The Post's* Outlook section on May 15, 1994. "No reasonable person would advocate military action in Haiti as a first choice," he wrote. "However, in the face of the ongoing brutalization of the Haitian people, Gen. Raoul Cédras and his cohorts are not leaving people of conscience any alternatives. Economically, politically and socially, the United States simply can no longer afford to appease the Haitian military."

In reporting on this article in the same newspaper three days later, columnist William Raspberry, who strongly supported Robinson's aims during his hunger strike, did not support his position this time. "War?" Raspberry asked himself. "I don't think so." This is indicative of the way the nation was split over Haiti in mid-1994.

A public opinion poll conducted by Time/CNN May 18 and 19 posed the question, "Thinking about the events taking place in Haiti, do you think the United States should send in military forces to oust the military rulers and install Aristide, or don't you think this way? The response was 68% in favor, 18% against and 14% not sure.

## William Gray Briefs Congress

On June 8, 1994, one month after being appointed by President Clinton as his special envoy to Haiti, William H. Gray spent 2 ½ hours briefing the U.S. House of Representatives Foreign Affairs Committee on U.S. policy toward Haiti. He covered progress made during his first month on the job, explained U.S. national interests in Haiti and outlined future U.S. strategy and intentions.

### First-month Progress

On May 21, 1994, as a consequence of U.S. leadership, UN Security Council Resolution 917 imposing stringent new sanctions on Haiti went into effect.

On May 26, Gray had met with President Balaguer of the Dominican Republic, together with Dante Caputo, UN/OAS envoy to Haiti, and reached an agreement to seal the border between the Dominican Republic and Haiti.

On June 3, 1994, the representatives of the Friends of Haiti in the United Nations (Argentina, Canada, France, the United States and Venezuela) decided to consider on a national basis expanded sanctions that would cut off commercial air traffic to and from Haiti and ban international financial connections with that country. They also expressed their determination to promote the full redeployment of a strengthened and reconfigured UN Mission in Haiti.

## Progress on Refugees

On May 19, Mr. Gray said, he and Mrs. Ogata, UN High Commissioner for Refugees, announced agreement on a plan for cooperation in the processing of Haitian refugees and locating countries for their settlement.

On June 1, the governments of Jamaica and the United States jointly announced a plan for shipboard processing of Haitian refugees in Jamaican ports.

On June 3, the government of the Turks and Caicos islands agreed to U.S. proposals for a land-based processing center on Grand Turk Island.

## Progress on Multilateral Cooperation

On June 6, together with U.S. Deputy Secretary of State Strobe Talbott, Gray attended a Meeting of Foreign Ministers of the Organization of American States in Belem, Brazil. A strong resolution was enacted which included a call upon all member states to assist in the resettlement of Haitian refugees, to support measures by the United Nations to strengthen the UN Military Mission in Haiti, and to support and reinforce existing and additional sanctions against the military regime in Haiti.

## U.S. National Interests in Haiti

Gray identified and discussed two basic interests of the United States in Haiti:

1. We have a moral stake in promoting democracy and human rights throughout the world.
2. The emergence of democracy as the prevailing form of government in this hemisphere is clearly and unmistakably in our self-interest.

## Strategy and Intentions

Gray defined the three principal future objectives of U.S. foreign policy in Haiti:

1. To bring about the prompt departure of the current military leadership in Haiti;
2. To provide additional due process to asylum seekers pending resolution of the crisis;
3. To mitigate human suffering in Haiti to the maximum extent possible.

## *Expanding the Sanctions*

On June 10, 1994 President Clinton announced the termination of all commercial air flights between the United States and Haiti, effective June 25, and the immediate prohibition of most private financial transactions between the two countries. A senior official said the additional steps were taken because the Haitian military leaders had shown no signs of leaving the country. "It's an indication that they need to get the message enforced," the official said. "We upped the pressure."

William Gray said the additional sanctions were targeted to have maximum effect on the coup leaders without causing additional damage to ordinary Haitians. From 65 to 75 percent of Haitian air traffic would be affected, he said. Canada announced that it would impose a separate ban on its commercial air traffic, and U.S. officials said that they hoped that France and the Netherlands, which provided most of the remaining service, would do likewise.

The financial sanctions extended beyond the freezing of assets, already in place, to the transfer of funds between the United States and Haiti, as well as Haitian financial transactions through the United States to third countries.

Following Clinton's announcement, the U.S. Department of State urged Americans in Haiti not involved in refugee relief to leave the country as soon as possible. It was also announced that the U.S. Embassy in Haiti would reduce its American staff and order the departure of the dependents of embassy employees.

Unfortunately lack of cooperation by some nations weakened the effect of the new sanctions. Canada and Panama suspended air service to Haiti, but Air France continued its three-flights-a-week schedule and said it might even replace its Boeing 737s with larger 747s.

On June 22, 1994, the United States expanded its freeze on U.S. assets of the Haitian military and its supporters to include all Haitians. But the United States had not yet cancelled the travel visas of wealthy Haitian civilians who had supported the coup. The Haitian military staged frequent parades and marches in Port-au-Prince to demonstrate to the people that they were still very much in control. They also played the card of nationalism, restricting the movements of foreigners, even declaring U.S. Senator Bob Graham of Florida *persona non grata* and vowing that the national flag would fly day and night over the National Palace until the current crisis was over. The televised World Cup soccer championship was continually interrupted by messages denouncing the embargo, and video replays of the 1915 U.S. invasion of Haiti.

Lt. Gen. Raoul Cédras withdrew $500,000 from Haiti's Central Bank, raising speculation (and some hope) that the move was in preparation for his leaving the country. Many of Haiti's wealthy families were feeling the crunch of the embargo and some were trying to persuade Cédras to resign as a step toward relieving the financial crisis.

## *Military Action Considered*

Call it invasion or intervention, peacemaking or peacekeeping, talk of some kind of forceful action to restore democracy to Haiti increased.

At the annual TransAfrica awards dinner June 4, the mood was one of impatience and frustration. Keynote speaker Representative Maxine Waters of California remarked, "I'd be happy if, tomorrow morning, the president said if the military leadership in Haiti doesn't leave by a certain date, we'll be coming on." Representative Kweisi Mfume of Maryland said, "Some of us feel there may be a need to do surgical strikes, simply to send a clear, unequivocal message to the military that the rape, mass murder and destruction can no longer be tolerated. Representative Donald Payne of New Jersey said, "We've got a man elected with 69% of the vote in a free election, and we're not helping him." Randall Robinson, executive director of the organization, called for a hemispheric force, ideally under the aegis of the United Nations, "to occupy Haiti and return Aristide to power." His call to arms was met with wild applause.

Meanwhile, the Clinton administration engaged in some long-range planning. It urged U.S. allies to pledge troops for a future 3,000-member peacekeeping force to maintain order once the military leaders of Haiti stepped down and Aristide was restored to office.

It would be different from the joint U.S.-Canadian military training mission contemplated under the Governors Island Agreement, which sought to disembark from the Harlan County in October 1993 but was prevented from doing so by armed thugs of the FRAPH organization. The force Clinton had in mind would actually take over some police duties while a police force meeting democratic standards was recruited and trained. It would protect Aristide and members of the government, human rights monitors and representatives of human rights organizations. It would also guard foreign embassies and protect infrastructure such as roads and water systems from attack or sabotage. In short, its purpose would be to prevent anarchy and civil war once the Haitian military leaders were removed from power.

The United States, Canada, France and Argentina were ready to contribute troops to this force, and there were expressions of support from several other OAS members.

While this force was planned for a post-liberation Haiti, Clinton did not discard the possibility of more immediate military intervention if required. Indeed, he repeatedly said that the military option remained on the table. By asserting that time was running out for the restoration of democracy in Haiti, he had left himself little alternative but to use military force if the top Haitian military leadership did not voluntarily step down. Senior officials said they wanted the crisis settled quickly, preferably before the end of summer.

Clinton was under considerable domestic pressure "to do something," not only from the Congressional Black Caucus but also from Governor Lawton Chiles of Florida because of a new wave of boat people resulting from the president's May 8 decision henceforth to give all intercepted refugees a chance to claim political asylum. A *Washington Post*/ABC News poll showed that 45% of the American people thought that the United States and its allies should take all necessary action, including the use of military force, to restore a democratic government to Haiti. This figure was up from 36% the previous month. Failure to remove Haiti's military leaders added to the mounting criticism of Clinton's capacity to conduct U.S. foreign policy. The same *Washington Post*/ABC poll indicated that while 41% of the American people disapproved his handling of foreign affairs in general, 45% disapproved of the way he was handling the situation in Haiti.

Department of Defense officials previously opposed to the use of military force in Haiti were giving the military option serious study. It was a tempting alternative, considering the weakness of Haiti's military forces. Contingency plans envisioned the use of 25-50,000 airborne, naval and special operations personnel and quick, positive results. The U.S. Senate, after a five-hour debate on U.S. Haitian policy, rejected 65-34 a resolution that would have required President Clinton to obtain authority from Congress before taking military action in Haiti. It later voted 93-4 to accept a non-binding resolution that said the president should seek the approval of Congress before committing U.S. troops to Haiti.

## *Shows of Strength*

In Haiti, provisional president Jonaissant reacted to all this saber-rattling by declaring a state of emergency, saying that the nation was in grave peril and under the threat of invasion and occupation. Under the Haitian constitution, the decree gave him the right to impose a curfew and restrict movement in order to guarantee public order, but it fell short of a declaration of a state of siege, which would have suspended all constitutional guarantees. In Washington, William Gray doubted that the measure would have any impact. In a show of "strength", the Haitian military leaders marched 150 infantry soldiers, with machine guns and an armored vehicle, through the streets of Haiti.

The United States conducted its own show of strength. It sent the 24th Marine Expeditionary Unit of 1,900 marines aboard four ships to Haitian waters. A typical MEU is equipped with 36 helicopters, two types of howitzers, light armored vehicles and amphibious assault vehicles — exactly what would be needed for an air and sea invasion of Haiti.

After their arrival, the marines conducted a mock evacuation on the nearby island of Grand Inaugua in the Bahamas, the kind of operation that would be carried out to evacuate Americans from Haiti in case of invasion.

The exercises were not conducted in secrecy. On the contrary they were accompanied by announcements and publicity so as to convince the Haitian military leadership that the United States was serious in its intention to intervene militarily in Haiti, and that it would be preferable for the leaders to step down on their own to avoid capture. But Army commander-in-chief Lt. Gen. Raoul Cédras remained defiant. He said he would resign only if the international community recognized the illegally installed provisional president, Emile Jonaissant, as the legal president of Haiti. Otherwise, he told the Associated Press, he would stay in power no matter what the consequences until his term as Army commander expired on January 31, 1995. Then he planned to run for president in elections the Jonaissant government was planning for early 1995.

## Invasion Preparations

U.S. officials stated that an invasion of Haiti was not imminent but the United States was prepared to use force if the broadened sanctions instituted in May did not produce the resignation of Haiti's top military leaders. In a briefing to congressional leaders on July 13, Secretary of State Warren Christopher said these individuals "do not have a license to stay on until the end of the year. . . . We think that the illegal government should go right now." He laid out what he termed the "very strong" American interests in Haiti: U.S. support for democracy in the hemisphere; maintaining stability in the region; prevention of the overthrow of democratically-elected governments; protecting the lives of several hundred Americans in Haiti; and stopping the massive refugee flow caused by conditions in Haiti.

In the meantime, the Haitian military moved to tighten its control over the civil population. First, the government ordered about 100 UN/OAS human rights observers to leave the country. They had been an embarrassment to the military during its conduct of its reign of terror in the country. Since January the group had reported 340 killings, 131 disappearances and 55 cases of politically-motivated rape. The last of these was particularly repugnant. When military thugs were unable to locate a particularly active Aristide supporter, they would enter that person's home and threaten to rape, or actually did rape his wife, daughter or girlfriend, often in full view of other members of his family held at gunpoint. Following the expulsion of the human rights observers, these and other abuses multiplied and went unreported. Death squads began dumping the corpses of dead persons on the streets with bones broken and bodies mutilated, as forage for pigs and dogs, and as a warning to others and their relatives. In some cases their faces were peeled to avoid their identification.

In the U.S. Congress, except for a few lawmakers who favored invasion, there were nearly as many positions on U.S. Haitian policy as there were members, but few were able to come up with an attractive alternative. The notable exception was Minority House Whip Newt Gingrich of Georgia, who proposed that the United States seize the small

Haitian island of Gonâve in the Gulf of Gonâve about 50 miles northwest of Port-au-Prince and install Aristide there, where he would have a base to operate pending his return to the capital itself.

Walter E. Fauntroy, a Baptist minister and liberal Democrat, former District of Columbia delegate to Congress and for 15 years chairman of a bipartisan task force on Haiti, said, "We're down to two choices. Either we go in or we walk away." He said his reluctant choice was to go in.

The United States started to lay the groundwork for a possible invasion. It asked the United Nations for its endorsement of U.S. military intervention in order to demonstrate to the world that such action by the United States had international support. U.S. preference was for a two-part resolution. The first part would authorize a military force to return Aristide to power. A coalition of forces from cooperating nations would be organized and led by the United States. Once they were able to establish a secure environment in the country, a UN peacekeeping force would take over to protect Aristide and reconstruct and retrain the Haitian army.

U.S. Congressman Bill Richardson of New Mexico visited General Cédras at his home in Haiti and sought to disabuse Cédras of the notion that the U.S. Congress was not behind the President's policies on Haiti. But Richardson's message was undermined in Washington by Senate Minority Leader Robert Dole. He kept raising the spectre of dead American soldiers being returned from Haiti to the United States in body bags.

Haitian Senator Bernard Sansaricq, a leading supporter of the coup against Aristide, said "We have always had not-so-open back-channel communications and fax exchanges with Dole and Helms and other Republican senators. We see Dole as someone who understands us, a friend of Haiti. We are delighted when he and others speak on our behalf." Sansaricq claimed that Haitian legislators who had supported the coup had communicated with Dole through Dole's foreign policy assistant, Randy Scheunmann, but Scheunmann denied any such contact. The anti-Aristide leaders of Haiti probably greatly over-estimated the amount of support they enjoyed in the U.S. Congress and other branches of the U.S. government, but the perception nonetheless became reality to them and emboldened them to cling to power.

# Chapter X

# UN-Sanctioned Intervention

On July 31, 1994, the long-awaited United Nations resolution to authorize the use of force by its member nations in Haiti (S/Res/ 940) was passed by the UN Security Council by a vote of 12 in favor and two abstentions. It gave approval to a U.S. plan to raise a multinational force to "use all necessary means to facilitate the departure from Haiti of the military dictatorship" and "establish and maintain a secure and stable environment on the understanding that the cost of implementing this temporary operation will be borne by the member states."

The resolution provided that the multinational force would terminate its mission when a secure and stable environment had been established in Haiti and that the United Nations Mission in Haiti (UNMIH) would take over for the purpose of (a) sustaining the secure and stable environment during the multinational phase and protecting international personnel and key installations, and (b) the professionalization of the Haitian armed forces and the creation of a separate police force.

The resolution also requested that the UNMIH also "assist the legitimate authorities in Haiti in establishing an environment conducive to the organization of free and fair legislative elections to be called by those authorities." It decided to increase the troop level of the UNMIH to 6,000 and established the objective of completing the UNMIH's work not later than February 1996.

Finally, the resolution specified that the UN Security Council would review sanctions against Haiti with a view of lifting them immediately after the return of President Aristide to Haiti.

Aristide backed S/Res/940 in a letter calling for prompt and decisive action to restore democracy in Haiti. He stated that the Haitian constitution barred him from giving more explicit support for foreign intervention. His letter had the effect of calming most countries of Latin America. Since Aristide was the legal president of Haiti, they could argue that they would not be a party to an unwanted, unilateral U.S. invasion.

Madeleine Albright, U.S. ambassador to the United Nations, said that the message to the three top military commanders was simple: "You can depart voluntarily and soon, or you can depart involuntarily and soon."

Though the resolution authorized the United States to raise a multinational force to enter Haiti, it provided that all expenses would be borne by the member states. This provision made it difficult for the United States to recruit allies for the operation unless the United States was prepared to underwrite their costs. Two weeks passed and only Argentina agreed to participate. Its contribution would be two warships that would remain outside the combat zone.

The United States was pleased to have Argentina cooperate, since its inclusion immediately had the effect of fulfilling the UN requirement that the force be multilateral. But the United States did not want too many different units from too many different nations because most military experts believed that this could complicate what most of them considered a rather simple operation against what was expected to be weak resistance. A coalition of forces would require joint planning, joint exercises and a joint command. The U.S. military felt it would be simpler and more effective to take complete charge, but understood the symbolic value of multilateralism.

In Haiti, General Raoul Cédras exuded non-chalance. Clad in blue jeans and a short-sleeved shirt, he spent Assumption Day, August 17, a major Haitian holiday, acting like a candidate for president. Cédras and his wife Yannick toured small towns with a large entourage, waving to sparse but enthusiastic crowds and chatting with politicians. The holiday marked not only the Roman Catholic celebration of the Assumption; it also marked the anniversary of the end of 19 years of occupation of Haiti by the U.S. Army in 1934. The Cédras show was designed to assure the common people that they did not have to fear a repetition of that invasion and occupation. The provisional president of Haiti, Emile Jonaissant, had called for elections in November, and it was widely believed Cédras would be able to maneuver to get himself elected to replace Aristide.

The United States increased its pressure on Cédras. When a prominent Roman Catholic priest, Reverend Jean-Marie Vincent, an active supporter of Aristide, was shot and killed outside his home on August 28, presumably by military gunmen, U.S. State Department spokesman Michael McCurry immediately put the blame on Haiti's military leaders, saying "your crimes only increase our outrage and strengthen our resolve to rid Haiti of your abuses. Make no mistake, outrages such as these reinforce the determination of the international community to take all necessary means to bring about the early restoration of democracy in Haiti." The words "all necessary means" were a euphemism for UN-sanctioned intervention.

## Invasion Plans Finalized

U.S. Deputy of State Strobe Talbott and U.S. Deputy Secretary of Defense John M. Deutch attended a meeting of the Caribbean Community in Kingston, Jamaica, and secured pledges from four of its members (Barbados, Belize, Jamaica and Trinidad and Tobago) to participate with a total of 266 troops in any future UN-sanctioned intervention in Haiti. U.S. troops would be in the first wave, with Caribbean soldiers following immediately to serve as military police. Antigua and the Bahamas said they would also consider participating.

The visit of Talbott and Deutch was *pro-forma* since the four nations that committed themselves had already agreed to do so in previous diplomatic communications. The number of troops was small but their participation lent an element of multilateralism to the prospective force. Their agreement sent a message to Cédras in nearby Haiti that the United States was indeed serious about removing the generals from power. Joint representation at the meeting by the deputy secretaries of the U.S. Departments of State and Defense also signaled to the world that there was no longer disagreement between their two departments on the need to invade Haiti if the top three Haitian military leaders refused to relinquish their posts.

At a joint press conference, Talbott and Deutch said the United States was determined to use force in Haiti, either to stabilize a democratic government after the military leaders left, or to drive them out of power. Deutch said, "there should be no question in anyone's mind that the multinational force is going to Haiti".

"If General Cédras and his colleagues are still in Port-au-Prince when the invasion force goes in," Talbott said, "I think it is dead certainty that they would be apprehended and, in due course, turned over to the legitimate government of Haiti."

Deutch said "the Haitian army and its backers would be making a serious mistake if they believed that the UN-sanctioned force would not go into Haiti in the near future. The only issues are the circumstances under which that force enters Haiti. It could be under permissive circumstances . . . or it could be under contested circumstances if the illegal government does not come to its senses and realize that the world is determined to see a change back to the elected government."

Deutch said the intervention would have overwhelming force so that if there is resistance it could be rapidly overcome and casualties minimized. But the best outcome, Deutch said, would be for the leaders to step aside so that the multinational force could quickly restore order and give way to UN peacekeeping units.

White House officials confirmed the Talbott-Deutch analysis. If U.S. entry into Haiti is peaceful, they said, U.S. forces would form part of an international force to restore President Aristide. If the Haitian generals did not step down voluntarily, the U.S.-led invasion would take place in October 1994.

Seven giant cargo ships were readied at U.S. ports around the nation to transport heavy equipment to U.S. landing forces, which were expected to number 15,000 for the first stage. One senior official said that a "drop dead date" by which Haiti's military leaders should leave had not yet been decided but the "window" was between the last week of September and mid-October. President Aristide would be restored to power during stage one.

Using about 1,800 U.S. marines already stationed off the coast of Haiti, the invasion could be carried out at short notice. The number of countries committed to participate had risen to ten — Argentina with two warships; Britain, which offered a frigate, a support vessel and police trainers; and eight Caribbean states — Antigua, Barbuda, the Bahamas, Barbados, Belize, Trinidad and Tobago, St. Vincent, and the Grenadines, which together were contributing a battalion.

Evidence that the United States was in final stages of preparation was deployment of the aircraft carrier Eisenhower to the Caribbean and an alert of the U.S. Army's 10th Mountain Division in Ft. Drum, New York. The USS Mount Whitney, an amphibious command ship, was ordered to Norfolk to be used as the headquarters for any landing on Haitian shores. The number of cargo ships held in reserve was increased from seven to twelve and the total number of troops from 15,000 to

20,000. It was foreseen that most of these troops would leave Haiti once the country was stabilized, when the United Nations would take charge in stage two, except for about 3,000 soldiers who would form part of the UN force, which would be led by a U.S. general. U.S. Secretary of State Warren Christopher announced that Belgium, the Netherlands and France had also agreed to participate in stage two.

On September 11, at Fort McNair in southwest Washington, top U.S. officials who would be involved in the UN-sanctioned intervention conducted a "walk-through" of planning for the invasion and its aftermath. On September 14, 700 paratroopers of the renown 82d Airborne Division at Fort Bragg, North Carolina conducted a practice jump to seize an airfield and evacuate Americans, in imitation of what might be their first task in leading an invasion of Haiti.

As the hour, still unknown, for the soon-expected intervention approached, political and military activity increased in both Washington, D.C. and Haiti. There was still some opposition in Congress to the use of U.S. military force in Haiti. Politicians and constitutional scholars debated whether the president had the authority to send U.S. troops into combat without congressional approval. The influential *Washington Post* editorialized against such action.

Finally, President Clinton decided to take his case to the American people. On September 15, 1994, in a televised address to the nation, he laid out the reasons for the planned intervention: that armed thugs can not be allowed to overturn the will of the people; that brutality against the people by the military regime in Haiti must stop; that the massive flow of Haitian refugees to the United States will not stop until democracy is restored to Haiti; that American credibility as a world leader is at stake. To Haiti's three principal leaders he said, "Your time is up; leave now or we will force you from power." The next day a *USA Today/ CNN/Gallup* poll showed that 56% of the American people said they supported an invasion.

In Haiti U.S. Ambassador William Swing was asked to deliver personal ultimatums to each of the three principal military leaders of Haiti: Lt. Gen. Raoul Cédras, Brig. Gen. Phillippe Biamby and Police Chief Michel Francois, to leave with U.S. assistance or face arrest when the U.S. military arrived. But Cédras, still defiant, said he was prepared to die for the Haitian people.

Whatever their final decision, U.S. forces would enter Haiti in a matter of days, U.S. officials said. If the leaders were still there, the military action would be a full-scale invasion to remove them. If they had left on their own, U.S. entry would be on the basis of "permissive planning," that is, by previous agreement with Haitian authorities. In order to cool expectations that the operation would be easy, Secretary of Defense William Perry warned that there could be casualties on both sides.

## *The Carter Mission*

At this point it was revealed by the White House that former U.S. president Jimmy Carter had been in communication with General Cédras for several months. Carter had known Cédras since he, Carter, had served as monitor of the 1990 election in which Aristide had been elected President of Haiti. Actually, the Carter connection was only one of several initiatives of this nature the Clinton administration had taken to persuade Haiti's top military leaders to discuss their departure from office. When the Carter contact bore fruit, the opportunity was seized immediately.

On September 16, President Clinton announced that a negotiating team composed of Carter, former chairman of the U.S. Joint Chiefs of Staff, Colin Powell, and Senator Sam Nunn, chairman of the U.S. Senate Armed Services Committee, would go to Haiti to seek a last-minute departure of the Haitian military leaders.

An administration official emphasized that the group had a mandate only to negotiate the *terms* under which Cédras, his assistant Brig. Gen. Phillippe Biamby and Police Chief Michel Francois would leave office, and nothing more. This official emphasized that the talks would be short and would not change the timetable for invasion. The administration had always said that U.S. forces would enter Haiti even if the leaders left voluntarily because their departure would leave a power vacuum which had to be filled in order to maintain law and order in the country.

The Carter delegation began meeting with Cédras in the afternoon of September 16. The subject was the timing of the military's agreement to leave power in relation to the entry of U.S. troops, i.e., which would come first; also the timing and conditions of transfer of both military and civilian power to U.S. forces.

On the second day, September 17, the Carter delegation made a courtesy call on retired general Herard Abraham who was army commander when Carter monitored the 1990 election. The delegation then met with the military high command, had dinner with a group of influential businessmen and met with members of parliament.

Without realizing it at the time, Carter was provided with the ultimate key to the success of his mission at the dinner with the Haitian businessmen. Former provisional primer minister Marc Bazin, who was present, warned Carter that he must talk to Yannick, Cédras' wife, who had been urging her husband to stand firm, and he offered to set up the meeting. Late that night, the U.S. delegation was invited to Cédras' home and spent more than an hour with Yannick explaining to her that the forced entry of U.S. military forces into Haiti would likely result in the loss of lives and that her own life and the lives of her children would be in danger. It was a very emotional meeting. At first Yannick expressed strong opposition to U.S. plans to use force, stood her ground, but finally relented. Given the strong influence she wielded over her husband, her shift in position undoubtedly was a major factor in Cédras' eventual agreement to "permissive entry" for U.S. forces.

The next morning, now in the third day, Carter, Nunn and Powell met with supporters of President Aristide, then had their first session with provisional president Jonaissant. At 11 a.m. they held another round of meetings with the military high Command which lasted nearly 6 ½ hours. At noon, the deadline for agreement passed, but Carter was able to secure a three-hour extension of the talks from President Clinton.

Cédras and Biamby attended all of the talks but Francois did not. As a lieutenant colonel, he was not a member of the high command. He had said, however, that he was prepared to accept whatever Cédras agreed to, including exile or dismissal from the army, if that proved necessary to reach an agreement. Carter phoned President Clinton several times on a secure line during the final round of discussions in order to keep him informed. Carter, Nunn and Powell kept stressing to Cédras that if he did not step aside peacefully he would be quickly ousted by a massive use of force.

What most concerned the military leaders was their personal security and that of the troops they would be leaving behind. Carter offered Cédras and Biamby two choices: either stay during the brief period between agreeing to resign and the arrival of the multilateral force, or not resign and face the possibility of personal harm to themselves and their families, plus destruction of the army. In brief, they could leave with honor and not appear to be capitulating, or they could flee and risk the consequences. Pentagon officials knew by early afternoon September 18 that an agreement was likely, but invasion plans were kept on schedule in order to place maximum pressure on the two generals.

At about 6:45 p.m. on September 14, 61 planes carrying paratroopers from the 82d Airborne Division left Pope Air Force Base in North Carolina, McGuire Air Force Base in New Jersey and Homestead Air Force Base in Florida, all bound for Haiti. The breakthrough in negotiations came when Biamby burst into the negotiating room holding a cellular telephone and told Cédras that he had just heard that the invasion was underway. Biamby insisted that the negotiations be broken off, but instead the negotiators crossed the street to the Presidential Palace to continue the talks with Jonaissant. With U.S. warplanes enroute and a 30-minute ultimatum from Clinton to sign, the Carter team faxed the text of a draft agreement to the White House. It was accepted by Clinton with the addition of a new provision which allowed the three military leaders to remain in office until October 15. Jonaissant signed the agreement without ceremony. Carter informed President Clinton, and the planes were recalled to their home bases 75 minutes after their departures, about one hour before their scheduled arrivals in Haiti.

At 9:30 p.m. President Clinton announced at the White House that General Cédras and his colleagues, Biamby and Francois, had agreed to leave their posts by October 15 and that the first U.S. troops would land in Haiti the next morning to smooth the way for the return of President Aristide. During this transition period, the Haitian military leaders pledged to cooperate with U.S. forces in joint operations to be conducted "with mutual respect."

Clinton said the military leaders might leave their posts earlier if granted amnesty by the Haitian parliament for their crimes. He said that Aristide would return after they resigned and that when this happened all economic sanctions against Haiti would be lifted immediately. There was no provision that required the military leaders to leave the country but it was expected they would. The agreement closely resembled the Governors Island accord of July 1993 in which the Haitian military leaders had agreed to leave their posts in October 1993 but failed to do so. This time U.S. Secretary of State Warren Christopher noted, 15,000 U.S. soldiers would be present to be sure they kept their promise.

On Haitian television just before midnight, provisional president Emile Jonaissant called for calm. "You can go to sleep," he told the people of Haiti, "knowing that there will be no invasion.

## *Early Landings*

At 9:30 a.m. on September 19, 1994, members of the U.S. 10th Mountain Division left the aircraft carrier USS Eisenhower aboard UH-60 Blackhawk helicopters and landed unopposed at the Main Gate of the International Airport at Port-au-Prince. It was the first contingent of 3,000 troops that entered Haiti that day as part of Operation Uphold Democracy, with a total of 15,000 scheduled to arrive by the end of the week.

The landing force was met by Brig. Gen. Jean-Claude Duperval, deputy commander of the Haitian army. Lt. Gen. Henry H. Shelton, leader of the intervention force, drove to Haitian military headquarters where he met with Lt. Gen. Cédras and Brig. Gen. Biamby. Coming out of the meeting, Shelton told reporters that Cédras had been very cooperative and that, in the interim pending their resignations, he and Biamby would be partners with U.S. forces in maintaining order. Shelton said that they had discussed methods and techniques they could use to lower the risks to American soldiers of violent confrontation with Haitian troops or their armed paramilitary units, known as *attachés*.

Shelton said that peacekeeping was not the primary goal of U.S. forces. So far as possible, he said, U.S. soldiers would stay out of conflicts between supporters of Aristide and the Haitian military. He said his forces would focus on Port-au-Prince for the first day, securing the city's port and airport, and then extend their presence to other areas. Army Maj. Gen. David Meade, who landed with Shelton, said U.S. troops were operating under peacetime rules of engagement, which meant fire only when fired upon, or if your life is threatened.

The first day was spent unloading equipment. There were no incidents. U.S. troops were welcomed everywhere but celebrations and public manifestations were muted for fear of inciting retaliation by the Haitian military. A highly sophisticated command center was set up aboard the USS Mount Whitney to coordinate the entire operation. The only real concern was the abuse of Haitian civilians by some in the Haitian military and how to prevent such abuse and still maintain their friendship and cooperation. The day could be considered a major success, especially when one remembers that radical adjustments in military planning had to be made in only nine night-time hours, from scheduled multiple midnight paratrooper drops by three airborne divisions, to early morning light infantry landings at Port-au-Prince International Airport by soldiers from the 10th Mountain Division.

The second day did not go so well. As Haitian celebrations of the arrival of American troops multiplied and intensified, actions by the Haitian police became hostile. In response to taunts and pro-Aristide chants and songs, they charged into crowds at the dock area and near the airport, carrying shields, tear gas cannisters, whips and clubs, some larger than a baseball bat. Those too slow to get out of their way received severe blows. At the main entrance to the port, a demonstrator trying to flee from a police charge tripped and was beaten to death. Another near the airport was killed under similar circumstances. In both cases U.S. soldiers were within 100 feet of the incidents, watched, but did nothing. All this took place in view of journalists and television cameras and was reported worldwide.

Inaction by U.S. soldiers in the face of murders by Haitian police of fellow Haitians drew criticism from many quarters. James O'Dea, director of the Washington Office of Amnesty International, said, "It is scandalous that U.S. troops are in this role coordinating with the Haitian military while people are bludgeoned in the streets." The United States was in the incongruous position of having to cooperate with the Haitian military even as their police killed their own people because of their excessive affection for President Aristide and the United States. In fact, during this transition period, the U.S. Agency for International Development was scheduled to pay their salaries!

Lt. Gen. Shelton was quick to take action. He called on Cédras and told him that the beatings of civilians had to stop. Cédras said he understood. In an interview with CBS television, Cédras said he told Shelton that Haitian authorities were taking measures to insure "that members of the public force have more self-control."

During Shelton's 80-minute meeting with Cédras, it was also agreed that a Haitian heavy weapons unit based at Camp d'Aplication, about six miles outside Port-au-Prince, would be rendered inoperable. Its weapons were destroyed, and its barracks were occupied by a U.S. Special Forces unit. The heavy weapons unit was the pride of the Haitian military and its elimination was the ultimate humiliation. Reports circulated that Cédras was considering leaving Haiti on October 12 in order to salvage some dignity for himself and his office by deciding his own date of departure from Haiti. At the same time, Police Chief Francois worked with the U.S. military police in an effort to control the apparatus of terror that he, himself, had built.

# U.S. Military Role Unclear

While Carter's agreement with General Cédras undoubtedly had the very favorable result of avoiding combat and bloodshed, the last-minute change in the military's mission, from subduing an enemy to cooperating with him, confused many of the troops. A different mindset was required, with little time for explanation and reorientation by commanders with respect to changed tactics and strategy and new rules of engagement. The "army thugs" that their Commander-in-Chief had described in his September 15 address to the nation had suddenly become persons with whom the U.S. military was expected to cooperate. During his briefing of President Clinton upon his return from Haiti, Carter told Clinton that he, Carter, had just received a telephone-call from his aide in Haiti, Robert Pastor, in which Pastor reported that all was going well and that the two generals, Cédras and Shelton, were riding around the city together in the same vehicle. Had the enemy become our friends?

At the beginning, the new rules of engagement provided that U.S. soldiers should not interfere in Haitian-on-Haitian violence but could and should act in their own defense or to prevent a general breakdown in civic order. The adverse reaction to the two killings in Port-au-Prince, when U.S. troops looked on and did nothing as Haitian police battered the victims to death, resulted in a change in the rules to permit action by individual soldiers in such cases. But each incident was a case unto itself, usually requiring prompt action, with little time for reflection, deliberation or analysis, not to mention consultation with one's superior for guidance. And language was almost always a barrier to communication with the native population.

A good example was the situation in Cap-Haitian. On September 19, some 1,500 U.S. marines landed at the airport in this, Haiti's second largest city, located on the north coast. Their greatest challenge was to prevent flag-waving crowds from smothering them with gratitude. A few Haitian soldiers also greeted them, carrying but not using their weapons. The only real concern of U.S. troops was the abuse of Haitian civilians by some members of the Haitian military and how to prevent it and still maintain their friendship and cooperation. Excellent relations with the community was established by loading the bare shelves of the city's general hospital with truckloads of medical supplies, converting it into the best equipped hospital in the country.

It was in Cap-Haitian, perhaps the most unlikely spot, that a firefight with casualties occurred. On the night of September 24, a marine patrol stopped in front of a police station where it appeared that civilians were being abused. One of the policemen raised his Uzi submachinegun as if to shoot. In the exchange of fire that followed, ten policemen were killed and a U.S. marine was slightly wounded.

The next day, emboldened by this action, hundreds of unarmed civilians stormed police stations and army barracks. The police and military had fled, leaving stocks of arms and ammunition behind. The rioters seized rifles and ran with them joyfully through the streets before turning them over to the marines. At one checkpoint, a marine reported that he had been given six machineguns and more than a dozen rifles. During the day hundreds of rifles and automatic weapons were turned over to the marines.

At four police stations, the crowds tore apart offices and scattered arrest records in the streets. Four hundred Haitian soldiers and policemen had left their posts. U.S. forces were caught between the Haitian police and military it sought to disarm and Haitian civilians seeking revenge. In nearby Gonaives, the situation was reversed. U.S. troops disarmed two paramilitary *attachés*, then had to rescue them from an angry mob.

The bodies of the ten policemen shot by the marines in Cap-Haitien were placed in body bags in a hospital morgue with no air-conditioning, then buried in a local cemetery. A few days later, their bodies were disinterred and reburied on the grounds of the Military Hospital in Port-au-Prince. This second funeral for the group was attended by provisional president Jonaissant, Cédras, Biamby and the rest of the high command. Haitian colonel Carl Dorelin, high command personnel officer, delivered a eulogy sharply critical of U.S. behavior toward Haiti.

## Congress Urges Withdrawal

Though the UN-sanctioned U.S. intervention was making good progress toward achieving its objectives, the "Bring-the-Boys-Home" syndrome so characteristic of U.S. participation in foreign wars in the Twentieth Century, was already sweeping over Congress, led by those who had not wanted U.S. soldiers to go to Haiti in the first place. Representative Newt Gingrich, House Minority Whip, announced that he would introduce a resolution calling for the U.S. military to get out of Haiti "at the most rapid possible speed." It sounded punitive, as though the military had behaved improperly. Several Senate Republicans predicted failure of the military operation, then only two days old. Sentiment mounted in both houses for setting some kind of deadline for withdrawal before Congress adjourned to campaign for elections set for November. Representative Robert G. Toricelli of New Jersey suggested invoking the War Powers Act to limit deployment to a maximum of 90 days unless Congress authorized an extension.

President Clinton, Secretary of Defense William Perry and Chairman of the Joint Chiefs of Staff, John Shalikashvili, urged Congress not to set a deadline. Perry said U.S. forces should remain in Haiti at least until early 1995 in order to insure fair parliamentary elections. "But I would not like to have a 'date certain' set," he said. "I think that complicates our operations. General Shalikashvili agreed. "Such a move would create its own dynamic and change things on the ground," he said.

Finally, just before adjournment, the House and Senate compromised on a resolution urging a "prompt and early withdrawal" of American troops from Haiti but set no date for the withdrawal. At that time the number of U.S. troops in the country had reached 19,600, with no indication that all would be "home for Christmas."

Congress failed to recognize that UN Security Council Resolution 940 already provided for a downsizing of U.S. forces in Haiti. When the UN Mission in Haiti would take over from U.S. forces in 1995, U.S. troops would be reduced to 3,000 and form part of a UN peacekeeping force of 6,000 under command of a U.S. general officer.

## *Tightening Security in Haiti*

The U.S. Department of State announced the arrival in Haiti of the first 26 of a planned 1,000 international police monitors from 29 countries for the purpose of watching for human rights violations and assisting in the training of a new Haitian police force separate from the military. Raymond W. Kelly, a former New York police commissioner, was chosen to head the group under contract with the Department of State. It would have a reporting function, he said, reporting on the conduct of individual officers, thus having an impact on who would ultimately remain in the police force.

About 500 more monitors, from Argentina, Jordan, Bolivia and St. Vincent, among other countries, were scheduled to arrive the following week, along with about 260 troops from Caribbean countries. The intervention was beginning to take on an international dimension. Up to this point, the United States had been the only active participant on the ground in Haiti.

In the closing weeks before President Aristide's scheduled return to Haiti on October 15, 1994, U.S. forces were mainly concerned with providing a secure environment for him to operate in the country. The parliament building was placed under heavy guard as its members, many returning with U.S. help after years of exile or from hiding, assembled and passed an amnesty bill, as provided for in the Carter agreement as a precondition to the resignation of Cédras, Biamby and Francois. Mayor Evans Paul came out of hiding and was returned to City Hall by U.S. troops. Other U.S. forces seized police stations across the country, including the notorious police headquarters, "The Cafeteria," where in the past pro-Aristide supporters brought in for questioning rarely left the premises alive. Where the Haitian police were permitted to operate, their behavior was closely monitored by the international police force which had been brought into Haiti for this purpose, In the words of U.S. Secretary of Defense William Perry, their duty was to monitor the conduct of the Haitian police "with the objective of affecting their behavior without assuming their responsibilities."

After crowds broke into warehouses in Port-au-Prince and Gonaives, U.S. forces provided guards for these buildings. They also closed down the main television station, which had been under military control and continued to broadcast strong anti-Aristide and anti-American propaganda.

To lessen the capacity for violence in the country, the U.S. Army began a program to buy back weapons, offering $50 for handguns, $100 for semi-automatic rifles, and $300 for heavy weapons. These were unrealistic prices in terms of average Haitian earnings but above black market prices, and such incentives were considered necessary to overcome the reluctance to give up weapons in such a violent society. Nevertheless, the first day's yield was meager: 19 pistols, 7 rifles, 2 submachine guns, 8 teargas grenades and 3 fragmentation grenades. As a result, the buy-back program took on the character of a foreign aid program.

September 30, 1994 was the third anniversary of the military coup which overthrew President Aristide. It is difficult to fathom why his followers considered this an occasion for celebration. Perhaps it was due to anticipation of their hero's return within 15 days, an emotion which they could not constrain. In any event, thousands of his followers poured out of a mass at Notre Dame Cathedral that morning waving

Aristide posters and clashed with armed men near the Normandie bar, a favorite gathering place for members of FRAPH, the military organization whose favorite indoor and outdoor "sport" was the murder of Aristide supporters. In skirmishes that lasted several hours, at least four demonstrators and one FRAPH gunman was killed. Dozens of U.S. soldiers were stationed a few blocks away in M551 Sheridan tanks and humvee all-terrain vehicles but did not intervene. Their deployment that day, at strategic crossroads leading to Petionville, was to protect the wealthy elite living there from attack by these same marchers. It illustrated once again the dilemma in which U.S. forces found themselves, of trying to prevent both violence of the military against Aristide supporters and violence of Aristide supporters against the military and their supporters.

The only positive results from the tragic event were instructions from Washington to the U.S. military to start disarming all paramilitary gunmen. The instructions were followed at once as U.S. troops searched for weapons at factories owned by prominent business families and detained four leaders of the notorious black-clad militia, the "ninjas," which served as a personal security force for General Cédras.

The greatest triumph of U.S. forces was the virtual destruction of FRAPH. On October 3, 1994, in a raid at its headquarters in Port-au-Prince backed by tanks, armored vehicles and helicopters, U.S. troops arrested 35 members of this nefarious organization, seized a large cache of weapons and then turned the buildings over to jubilant crowds that promptly tore them apart and destroyed their furnishings. Similarly, U.S. forces raided FRAPH headquarters in Cap-Haitien and detained 75 persons.

At the time of Aristide's return to Haiti, the United States exercised all civil as well as military control of Haiti, and the nation enjoyed peace and stability for the first time since the coup which had caused his departure.

# Chapter XI

# Aristide and Democracy Restored

P resident Clinton was clear and consistent in his articulation of the core of U.S. policy toward Haiti. He summed it up in seven simple words which he repeated on many occasions: to restore Aristide and democracy to Haiti. The physical restoration of Aristide proved easy, since the United States controlled the country. It involved little more than providing him and his entourage security and air transportation from Andrews Air Force Base near Washington, D.C. to the international airport in Port-au-Prince, and from the airport to the National Palace. What turned out to be a much greater challenge was the task of restoring the semblance of democracy in a nation where it had existed for only a short time and never had deep roots.

## *Major Changes*

President Aristide sought to set the tone for his return to Haiti in a speech before the United Nations on October 4, 1994. He spoke about a "festival of reconciliation, democracy and peace. . . . We are going to prepare the coffee of reconciliation in the filter of justice, so that there will be no trace in it of violence or vengeance."

He pointed out that under the Haitian constitution he could not authorize full amnesty to Haiti's military leaders. Under the Haitian constitution, he said, such amnesty could cover "political crimes" but not criminal offenses. He gave oblique recognition to the U.S. role in the liberation of Haiti when he said, "Together, President Clinton and I have opened a tunnel through so much suffering." He received a standing ovation.

In a press conference that followed his speech, Aristide said that he was satisfied that U.S. troops had begun to disarm paramilitary gunmen in Haiti. He pledged a restructured and reduced force of about 1,500 soldiers, while a separate police force would number about 10,000. He said he would immediately launch a national literacy campaign and an effort to persuade more doctors to take care of the poor. He promised to plant 6 million trees a year to replace those cut by peasants for making charcoal. He called for new foreign investment and summoned Haitian exiles to return to their homeland. He promised to step down from office when his constitutional term would end with the inauguration of a new president on February 7, 1996.

Aristide's understanding of the scope of amnesty under the Haitian constitution was confirmed three days later by the passage of an amnesty bill by the Haitian parliament. It provided for a political amnesty for leaders of the coup that toppled Aristide from power but left open the possibility that Cédras, Biamby and Francois might one day be prosecuted for common crimes, such as murder, rape or corruption.

On October 4 Francois fled to the Dominican Republic. On the same day, Emmanuel Constant, leader of the terrorist organization FRAPH, whose headquarters had recently been ransacked by followers of Aristide, read a speech in English drafted by U.S. embassy officials, in front of the National Palace and under protection from an angry crowd by U.S. military police. He renounced violence and promised to cooperate with Aristide. "Violence no longer has a place in our society." he said. "I'm asking everyone to put down their stones, their tires and their guns." On October 8, 1994 Biamby tendered his resignation, which was accepted by Cédras the following day.

Cédras himself resigned in a brief ceremony on the steps of military headquarters on October 10, 1994. He was protected from jeering crowds by U.S. troops, whose commander, Lt. Gen. Shelton, joined him on the podium. Cédras handed over his ceremonial command flag to his deputy commander, Maj. Gen. Jean-Claude Duperval, who immediately became acting commander-in-chief.

Cédras' resignation speech was quite conciliatory. To his troops he said, "Today, at our side, we have the U.S. military. The U.S. military has told us they have come here to create a new nation, and therefore you should place yourself beside them. I will not be with you. I have decided to leave the country for your protection, so that my presence will not be a motive to create terror and destabilization against the military. You have no right to be doubtful or despair. The U.S. military is helping us to rebuild our country. I ask you to cooperate."

As Cédras made his speech, the roar of the hostile crowd virtually drowned out his voice. Thousands of people danced around the headquarters in joyous celebration, many shouting pro-Aristide slogans, waving U.S. flags and ridiculing the small group of Haitian soldiers gathered to hear the speeches. About a dozen U.S. armored vehicles and scores of U.S. troops surrounded the crowd, the podium and the Haitian soldiers.

General Duperval was also conciliatory. "We need to build an army that is unified, that is disciplined, that has respect for life and human rights," he said. Like Cédras, he praised General Shelton, saying to the Haitian troops, "We will benefit from the experience and leadership of our American colleagues. We shall be working together with them."

As the ceremony broke up, many in the crowd shouted obscenities at the departing Haitian soldiers but warmly cheered American troops as they withdrew. As Cédras drove off, crowds surged around his vehicle. Shots were fired in the air, presumably by the general's security detail, to ward off the demonstrators. At some point a rock smashed the rear window of the vehicle.

With the resignation of Cédras and Biamby, the next task was to get them out of the country before October 15, the scheduled date for Aristide's return. The United States found itself in the role of facilitating the exile of two men that President Clinton had condemned as armed thugs just a month before, of even providing financial and other incentives for their quick departure, with 23 of their relatives and associates.

After some shopping around, the United States was able to persuade Panama to receive the two generals and their entourage. The United States even provided them a private jet for a scheduled departure at 10 p.m. on October 12. But the plane did not depart until 3 a.m. on October 13. The United States had committed itself to renting three luxury properties that Cédras was leaving behind, and most of the five hours were spent haggling over a fair rental price. While the jet sat on the runway and U.S. soldiers served as baggage handlers, the terms of each contract were painstakingly negotiated. One diplomat reported that Cédras' wife, Yannick, conducted the negotiations. The men, he said, were unable to make decisions. They were in a state of shock. The total rent finally agreed upon for the three properties was $12,000 a month. It was paid in advance for six months or a year, depending on the property, in order to provide Cédras with spending money when he arrived in Panama.

The United States also agreed to release the frozen assets of the three former Haitian commanders, allowing them to keep millions of dollars they had illegally amassed during their brutal rule, much of it through drug smuggling, black marketing or profiteering from the sale of smuggled basic products during the embargo. Cédras had been living a life of luxury and was estimated to have amassed more than $100 million while receiving an official salary of only $900 a month. Biamby, who had led a more austere life and had passed much of his gains to troops under his command, was believed to have saved several million. When they arrived in Panama, the group occupied an entire floor of a luxury Panama City hotel and was scheduled to reside in seclusion on the nearby Pacific resort island of Contadora.

In Haiti, provisional President Jonaissant announced his resignation, and U.S. troops occupied the Presidential Palace and government ministry buildings in preparation for Aristide's return. So that the government would not be paralyzed in the interim, caretaker Prime Minister Robert Malval agreed to serve as head of government, but only until Aristide arrived. All ministry buildings had been looted, and U.S. troops, after the fact, provided for their security.

Despite, or perhaps because of, celebrations by Aristide's followers, the political climate was not ideal for his return. To the wealthy elite, he represented their fear of the poor masses. Many of them had hidden semi-automatic weapons in case of need to protect themselves. Haitian radio reported that Major Mare Valvue, the Haitian army officer in charge of security at the airport where Aristide was scheduled to land, was replaced after he threatened to "blow Aristide's brains out" as soon as he arrived. A week before his arrival, a bus driven by a partisan of the military regime purposely ran down a crowd of several hundred Aristide supporters, killing at least 14 and severely injuring a dozen more. The U.S. Drug Enforcement Agency continued its investigation of cocaine trafficking in Haiti, an inquiry which reportedly involved the new chief of the Haitian armed forces, Maj. Gen. Jean-Claude Duperval. And nearly a year after U.S. forces had entered Haiti, the United States and Haiti had not yet signed a Status of Forces Agreement to define the role of U.S. forces in the country. The only positive note was a major effort, organized by Port-au-Prince mayor Evans Paul, to clean the streets of the city before Aristide arrived.

## *Restoring Aristide*

Saturday, October 15, 1994, was a major day in the life of Haitian President Jean-Bertrand Aristide. On that day, he moved from his one-room apartment in downtown Washington, D.C. to his presidential office at the National Palace in Port-au-Prince, Haiti. It was not an ordinary move but a triumphant return, as president of his native land which he had been forced to leave as a result of a military coup three years before. It was the first time in Haitian history that an exile ruler had ever returned to office.

The evening before his departure, Aristide was given a farewell reception by President Clinton at the White House, at which Aristide thanked the United States for its hospitality during his years of exile in Washington and the president congratulated him for his pending return and wished him well. Aristide left early the next morning accompanied by Secretary of State Warren Christopher and Afro-American activists, including Jesse Jackson, members of the Congressional Black Caucus, and Randall Robinson, executive director of TransAfrica, whose hunger strike the previous spring had led to major changes in U.S. policy toward Haiti.

The entire group filled three planes and arrived at the airport in Haiti at 12:15 p.m. They were met by General Shelton and were immediately ferried by a fleet of ten Blackhawk helicopters to the National Palace. There Aristide, dressed in a black suit, wearing a giant red and blue gold-fringed sash of office, and standing behind a transparent bullet-proof glass shield before an estimated 10,000 persons, threw a white dove in the air, to the wild cheers of the crowd.

The theme of his speech, which he delivered in French, English and Creole, and repeated many times, was, "No to violence, no to vengeance, yes to reconciliation." Never, never, never, never again, he said, will one more drop of blood flow. "Let us live in peace, All guns must be silent. . . . There will be security in the morning, security at noon, security at night." His speech was filled with praise for American forces and his every word was cheered loudly by the jubilant crowd before him.

In New York, the United Nations Security Council lifted all economic sanctions that had been imposed on Haiti. Its resolution expressed "confidence that the people of Haiti can now rebuild their country with dignity and consolidate democracy." It also reaffirmed "the willingness of the international community to provide assistance to the Haitian people." The removal of sanctions was made effective as of 12:01 a.m. October 16.

## *Democracy Restored*

Did the act of restoring Aristide to Haiti also simultaneously restore democracy to Haiti? It certainly did in contrast to the cruel military dictatorship that held sway during his three-year absence. With equal certainty, it can be said that Aristide's return alone did not and could not magically transform the Haitian political system to a vibrant democracy. Aristide, himself, was not a model democrat. Change to democracy would require great effort by a great number of people over a considerable period of time. Two centuries of authoritarian tradition would have to be overcome.

The most favorable appraisal of the situation at that time was that Aristide's return provided the inspiration to work toward the reestablishment of democratic government. Aristide had learned a great deal about the functioning of American democratic institutions during his three-year exile in Washington. He had returned to Haiti with different perspectives on the function of government.

In this section we will examine the early efforts of Aristide to re-establish democracy in the Haitian nation and appraise the success of such efforts, bearing in mind that the perfect democracy has never existed anywhere and that Aristide and the Haitian people were and still are burdened by the albatross of nearly two hundred previous years of authoritarian rule and brutal dictatorship.

To assess progress toward democracy requires some standard of measurement. First, we need an acceptable definition of democracy. The highly respected *American Heritage Dictionary* lists no less than *five* definitions of democracy:

1. Government of the people, exercised either directly or through elected representatives.
2. A political or social unit that has such government.

3. The common people, considered as the primary source of power.
4. Majority rule.
5. The principles of social equality and respect for the individual within a community.

Lyman Tower Sargent, a renowned political theorist, in his book, *Contemporary Political Ideologies* (The Dorsey Press, Chicago, 1987), lists and discusses seven key elements of democracy:

1. Citizen involvement in decision making.
2. Some degree of equality among citizens.
3. Some degree of liberty or freedom granted to or retained by citizens.
4. A system of representation.
5. Rule of law.
6. An electoral system — majority rule.
7. Education.

Let us now examine the extent to which President Aristide addressed these criteria during the first few months following his return to Haiti and the extent to which progress was made toward their fulfillment.

## 1. Citizen Involvement

Participatory democracy was not a part of Haitian political tradition and there were no signs that it was encouraged by Aristide. The political tradition over the years was to take to the streets, usually in groups, and for the three preceding years all democratic demonstrations had been broken up by violent means by the military regime or paramilitary groups. Citizens organizations that might have become centers for resistance were routinely prohibited by the military government, particularly in the rural areas. The only effective private organization that operated during the Cédras era was a human rights monitoring group under the tutelage of Jean-Claude Bayeaux, a former professor of the University of Puerto Rico, who had returned to Haiti to help his countrymen. As a consequence of his efforts, he received many death threats. Fortunately, with the return of Aristide, the raison d'être for his organization ceased. Human rights were respected.

## 2. Equality Among Citizens

Inequalities between the rich and the poor were disturbing to Aristide as a parish priest and equally so during his first eight months as president of Haiti. At that time his rhetoric was inflammatory and bordered on a call for class warfare. Three years in the United States, where he became acquainted with the U.S. tax structure and public assistance programs for the needy, mellowed his outlook. He became convinced that at least some of the gap between the rich and poor could be bridged through democratic measures such as tax reform, job creation, expansion of public assistance, humanitarian aid and, if necessary, welfare assistance.

The first of these claimed most of his attention. He was determined to move quickly to oblige wealthy Haitians to pay a greater share of the tax burden. A great number of tax exemptions existed for the rich, and tax evasion was pervasive. Aristide was more concerned with tax collection than he was with new taxes or tax increases. He was also concerned with creating jobs for the poor and for soldiers dismissed as a result of down-sizing the Haitian armed forces. He also sought a broad expansion of public service: nutrition services, well-equipped clinics and hospitals and improved and more economic public transportation. He sought to bring living standards for the poor closer to those of the rich.

Aristide came around to the view that the best way to create jobs and eradicate poverty was to create an environment in which the private sector could flourish. He came to realize that the only hope for bringing democracy and economic justice to the island was to win the cooperation of the wealthy classes. To reassure the business community of his commitment to free enterprise and respect for public property, he invited 490 Haitian businessmen to the National Palace for a dialog. More than 400 accepted, and the exchange of views was cordial and beneficial. Fritz Mevs, scion of one of the wealthiest families in Haiti, who had previously opposed Aristide, actually proposed that Aristide's mandate be extended for three years beyond the constitutional limit of February 1996 in order to compensate Aristide for the three years he was forced to spend in exile.

## 3. Liberty and Freedom

The lack of liberty and freedom in Haiti prior to the assumption of presidential powers by Aristide in 1991 and during the three years of dictatorship that followed his removal from power by a coup d'etat, was not due to the lack of guarantees in the Haitian constitution. On the contrary, the framers of that constitution were determined to avoid a repetition of the kind of dictatorship represented by Francois Duvalier and his son, Jean-Claude. Accordingly, they enumerated a full range of liberties, freedoms and rights in the constitution they forged in 1987.

The Haitian Constitution of 1987, still valid today, contains a preamble and ten sections which together set forth in great detail the rights and freedoms of the Haitian people. The purpose of the constitution, itself, according to its preamble, is to insure the "inalienable and imprescriptable rights of life, liberty and the pursuit of happiness" for the Haitian people; to implant democracy, "which entails ideological pluralism and political rotation and affirms the inviolable rights of the Haitian people;" to eliminate "all discrimination between the urban and rural populations . . . by recognizing the right to progress, information, education, health, employment and leisure for all citizens;" and "to set up a system of government based on fundamental liberties, and respect for human rights, social peace, economic equity, concerted action and participation of all the people in major decisions affecting the life of a nation."

The ten sections, all under Chapter II, guarantee right to life and health, individual liberty, freedom of expression, freedom of conscience, freedom of assembly and association, the right to an education, freedom to work, the right to private property, the right to information and the right to security.

Some of these "rights," "liberties" and "freedoms" sound more like economic and social wishes than political guarantees, but they all have in common the fact that they were routinely violated by the Cédras dictatorship. That the return of Aristide offered hope for change is attested by the fact that by early 1995 all of the 21,400 Haitian refugees at Guantanamo Bay, Cuba, had returned to Haiti, nearly all of them voluntarily.

## 4. A System of Representation

The Haitian constitution provides for a bicameral legislature consisting of a Senate and a House of Deputies. Members of both chambers are elected by direct suffrage and majority vote in their districts. During Aristide's exile, this legislature, usually referred to as the parliament, met irregularly, usually when convened by Cédras to serve his own purposes. At the time of Aristide's return it was functioning well, having just approved an amnesty as a prerequisite for Cédras' resignation. New elections for parliament were expected sometime during 1995.

## 5. Rule of Law

Maintaining law and order was the severest challenge for President Aristide on his return, and he had to rely on the U.S. forces for help. Law and order on the streets was the highest priority and Aristide dedicated most of his efforts in this area to building and training a new police force. A separate police force did not yet have a legal basis, since parliament had not yet passed a law separating the police from the army. Nevertheless, because of the urgency to control street violence, it was decided to proceed with formation of the force and to leave formal separation to a later date.

About 1,200 physically fit Haitian refugees were recruited from camps at the Guantanamo Naval Station on the assumption that they would be among the most loyal to Aristide. A program for recruiting, screening and training, or retraining cadets for this new police force was begun by the U.S. Department of Justice. Former New York City police Chief Raymond Kelly was placed under contract with the U.S. Department of State to direct a 20-nation monitoring team assigned to supervise the trainees once they were assigned street duty.

The first class of 334 Haitian policemen graduated on October 29 after a brief course on the fundamentals of law enforcement ethics and non-violent crowd control. Lt. Col. Pierre Estander was named commander of this new force. The goal was to create a police force that would be respected rather than feared. In practice, U.S. military forces carried out the basic responsibility for securing law and order in the country until they could be replaced by the United Nations Mission in Haiti, as called for by UN Security Council Resolution 940 of July 31, 1994.

On November 17, 1994, President Aristide appointed a new army commander, Brig. Gen. Bernardin Poisson, as part of his plan to legitimize and transform Haiti's disgraced army without completely disbanding it. Until that time Poisson had held a low-profile post as a colonel in charge of the fire department.

One troublesome question which haunted Aristide upon his return to Haiti was what to do with the Haitian army. Should he disband it altogether, replace it with a constabulary on the model of Costa Rica, or continue it on a reduced scale. U.S. military and intelligence officials pressured him to preserve the army intact as an institution. A group of U.S. military officers worked with pro-Aristide military officers to screen out officers with records of dishonesty or human rights abuses, discharging some and assigning others abroad as military attachés.

As a result of a six-week sweep by U.S. forces, the guns distributed by Haiti's military leaders were largely off the streets, and only the police were authorized to carry firearms.

To many followers of Aristide, his continuing campaign for reconciliation clashed with the need to establish justice in the nation. Many thought the army and police should be punished for their crimes, to deter their repetition. After the financial incentives given to Generals Cédras and Biamby to encourage their departure, many felt that the army was being rewarded rather than punished for their crimes. One problem in rendering justice, however, was the lack of a reliable, non-political judicial system in the country after three years of military "justice" and "street justice."

## 6. An Electoral System and Majority Vote

Article 191 of the Haitian constitution provides for a Permanent Electoral Council responsible for "organizing and controlling with complete independence all electoral procedures throughout the territory of the Republic." Deputies and Senators are elected by a majority of votes cast in primary assemblies. Because of irregularities committed during the Cédras dictatorship, plans were begun for parliamentary elections in 1995. The first step was the organization of a provisional Electoral Council for this purpose.

## 7. Education

In Haiti as elsewhere, an educated electorate was considered a prerequisite for effective democracy. Thus, the right to an education was written into the 1987 constitution and article 52-1 of this constitution obligates all citizens to educate themselves. However, the school system deteriorated seriously during the period of the embargo. Many children were malnourished and others were kept out of school to work and supplement family income. The illiteracy rate was placed at 75%.

Upon the return of Aristide, the international community began a widespread program of assistance to improve Haitian schools. UNICEF offered $3 million for the purchase of materials and for scholarships for 150,000 students. The United States planned to assist in the training of 10,000 teachers and 25,000 students. Canada committed itself to providing $5 million for the purchase of books and for the repair of schools and dispensaries. Aristide announced that $250,000 would be dedicated to the construction of a university center on property previously confiscated from the exiled dictator, Jean-Claude Duvalier.

In summary, while the 1987 Haitian constitution established an excellent framework for the restoration of democracy in Haiti, a long road lay ahead toward full realization of these mandates in practice and the establishment of effective democracy in the country. By 1995, however, a good start had been made. Aristide had chosen his prime minister and cabinet. A start had been made toward professionalization of the Haitian army and police. U.S. Defense Secretary William Perry said that U.S. troops had rounded up 14,000 weapons through searches and gun purchases. The army and police and their civilian extensions, FRAPH, rural bands, *attachés*, etc., were no longer terrorizing the country. Plans were made for holding new parliamentary elections and for the transfer of peacekeeping efforts from the United States to the United Nations mission in Haiti. The United States would then be able to reduce its military forces in the country to 2,400 troops which it had committed itself to contributing to this UN force of 6,000.

The real bellweter as to whether democracy is restored in Haiti will be the creation of a new army and police force under secure civilian rule and secondly, since a sitting president is constitutionally ineligible to succeed himself, whether elections for president are free and fair in November 1995 and whether the transfer of power from Aristide to a successor on Inauguration Day, February 7, 1996, will take place in a peaceful manner.

# Chapter XII

# Lessons in Conflict Resolution

The crisis in Haiti from 1991 to 1994 was essentially a conflict over who had the right and authority to govern the people of that nation. Was it President Jean-Bertrand Aristide, elected by two thirds of the voters of that country in an election deemed fair and free by all neutral observers, or the military junta that ousted him from office, forced him into exile and seized control of all decision-making power in that nation?

Aristide had the backing of the vast majority of the Haitian people and the support of the entire international community. The junta had the support of the army, police and wealthy elite of Haiti, but little or no support outside the country. The conflict was finally settled through a combination of conventional and non-conventional diplomacy and the use of outside military force sanctioned by the United Nations.

This chapter reviews six specific kinds of action undertaken by the international community to restore Aristide to power, evaluates the success of each, and draws lessons from the experience which may be useful in helping to resolve crises of this type in the future.

## Use of Conventional Diplomacy

Diplomacy came into play the same morning that the coup against President Aristide took place. As soon as OAS Secretary General Joao Baena Soares learned what happened, he called a meeting of the OAS Permanent Council pursuant to OAS General Assembly Resolution 1080 of June 5, 1991. The Council unanimously condemned the coup and resolved to call an ad hoc Meeting of Foreign Ministers of the organization. This meeting took place on October 2, 1991. It was addressed by President Aristide, who recommended that an OAS delegation be sent to Haiti as soon as possible to explain the organization's position to the coup leaders.

The Foreign Ministers passed a resolution condemning the coup and another authorizing a civilian mission to Haiti to reestablish democracy in the country. Baena Soares led the mission, which was composed of the Foreign Ministers of seven member states plus U.S. Assistant Secretary of State for Inter-American Affairs Bernard Aronson. The mission held two days of meetings with the coup leader, General Cédras, but made no progress in resolving the crisis. At an OAS Foreign Ministers meeting on October 8, 1991 a resolution was passed urging all member states to freeze Haitian government assets and impose an embargo on trade with Haiti.

On November 23, 1991 Columbian Foreign Minister Augusto Ramirez chaired a meeting between Aristide and leaders of the Haitian parliament in Cartagena, Columbia, but again no progress was made.

The OAS made another effort at mediation early in 1992 when it arranged a meeting in Washington, D.C. between Aristide and René Theodore, a prominent politician from Haiti. After three days of negotiations an eight-point agreement was made whereby Aristide would name Theodore Prime Minister and Aristide would return to Haiti and grant an amnesty to all persons involved in the coup. The agreement was roundly applauded by the OAS negotiators in Washington but was deemed unconstitutional by the Haitian Supreme Court. The only agreement successfully brokered by the OAS was one between Aristide and the puppet Haitian prime minister Marc Bazin which provided for the stationing of 18 OAS observers in Haiti to help reduce human rights abuses.

The United Nations began to take interest in the Haitian issue and reached agreement with the OAS to appoint Dante Caputo, former Argentine foreign minister, as the official OAS/UN representative for negotiations with the Haitian military government. Caputo, a skilled diplomat, traveled widely around Haiti and spoke to everyone in the decision-making process. He secured the agreement of Cédras and Bazin to deploy additional human rights monitors to Haiti and to reopen talks on restoring democracy to the country. Perhaps his greatest triumph was to persuade Cédras and Aristide to agree to talks at Governors Island, New York, that resulted in a ten-point agreement between the two men designed to resolve the issues between them.

The agreement had many flaws, as described in Chapter VI. It broke down when Cédras engineered violence which prevented the landing in Haiti of a small contingent of unarmed U.S. and Canadian technical specialists as provided in Section 5c of the agreement. Cédras refused to meet with representatives of the "Four Friends of Haiti" (Canada, France, the United States and Venezuela) to revive the agreement.

U.S. diplomatic activity picked up with the appointment of former U.S. Congressman William H. Gray as U.S. special envoy to Haiti. Together with Dante Caputo, he was able to reach agreement with President Balaguer of the Dominican Republic on sealing that country's border with Haiti. He was also able to reach agreement with the UN High Commissioner for Refugees on the processing of Haitian refugees and their settlement in other countries.

Some of the best efforts to advance U.S. policy toward Haiti were conducted at the United Nations by U.S. Ambassador Madeleine Albright. The U.S. Embassy in Haiti also played an important role in supporting U.S. policy in Haiti by maintaining pertinent U.S. agencies and departments informed on events in the country and carrying out instructions of the U.S. Department of State.

## Lessons Learned

The limitations of regional multilateral diplomacy were revealed in unsuccessful efforts by the Organization of American States to resolve the Haitian conflict. The use of a single, highly-skilled roving emissary, Dante Caputo, as simultaneous negotiator for both the OAS and the United Nations aided the coordination of policy between these two organizations. However, Caputo met his Waterloo at Governors Island, New York, when he did not allow sufficient time nor have sufficient staff to guarantee a well-thought-out agreement between President Aristide and General Cédras.

In summary, multilateral diplomacy is difficult and complex. When two organizations hold a common position, they can be more effectively represented by a single skilled diplomat responsible to the Secretaries-General of the two organizations. Bringing the two principals in a dispute together in a quiet, isolated environment to hammer out an agreement between them can be effective but such a conference must be carefully structured, as well as the agreement itself, preferably with a protocol for enforcement.

## *Use of Embargoes and Sanctions*

Embargos and sanctions of various kinds were levied against Haiti throughout most of the period of the Haitian crisis, 1991-1994. Within eight days of the coup which deposed Aristide, and immediately after the failure of the OAS civilian mission to Haiti, that organization urged its members to freeze Haitian government assets in their countries and cease all trade with Haiti except humanitarian aid. Three days later the United Nations appealed to members to support OAS resolutions on Haiti and so, by implication, those imposing an embargo and sanctions. It wasn't until June 23, 1993 that the United Nations imposed a world-wide embargo of its own.

This action brought Cédras to the conference table at Governors Island, where he succeeded in getting a provision to lift the embargo inserted as step 4 of the agreement. As soon as Robert Malval was installed as prime minister of Haiti, he asked the United Nations to suspend its sanctions. The United Nations did so, freeing Cédras to continue his violence against the followers of Aristide. When Cédras violated step 5c of the agreement by thwarting the docking of the Harlan County, the United Nations reimposed its oil embargo on Haiti and froze the financial assets of all the Haitian military leaders involved in that incident. The United States imposed its own financial and travel restrictions on about 100 Haitian military officers and their supporters.

A trend began to develop with respect to the administration of sanctions. They were no longer exclusively directed at Haiti as a whole but some began to be targeted against specific individuals or groups of individuals. But the general embargo continued and President Clinton sent six naval vessels to Haiti to enforce it.

The embargo had some undesirable side effects. It made the poor poorer and the rich richer, particularly the military against whom it was directed. The rich made additional profits from smuggling contraband items, particularly petroleum products. At the United Nations, Aristide called for a total embargo against Haiti, but he was contradicted by his own prime minister, Robert Malval, who said it would be a heavy burden for the country.

There was no doubt that the embargo had a devastating effect on the country. Yet the United Nations Security Council, pressed by the United States, approved a near-total global embargo on Haiti, as well as financial and travel restrictions on Haiti's military leaders. They were not to be lifted until the leaders stepped down from office and Aristide was restored. On June 10, 1994 President Clinton announced the termination of all commercial flights between the United States and Haiti and prohibition of most private transactions with that country.

## Lessons Learned

1. Embargos and sanctions are double-edged swords. They must be carefully targeted to achieve the desired results. Otherwise they can have disastrous effects on people you want to help and enrich those you want to penalize.
2. An embargo is difficult to enforce and is easily circumvented. Continuous vigilance by sea, land and air is required to prevent violations.
3. Embargos can have unfortunate side effects. For example, each upward racheting of the embargo against Haiti led to a new wave of refugees leaving the country for the United States.
4. Embargos bring out the best and the worse in people. On the one hand they bring families and neighbors together to share suffering and scarce commodities. Humanitarian organizations did heroic work with limited resources in relieving hunger and illness among the poor. On the other hand, embargos can bring out greed. Few persons can resist the temptation to make huge profits through smuggling contraband.
5. The effects of an embargo can be devastating. Embargos can cause unemployment, food shortages, famine, even death among the innocent. It is impossible to save a country by destroying it.
6. Embargos must be carefully targeted to those on whom one wishes to exert pressure.
7. Each participant in an embargo must play his part fairly. It was unjust for France to permit Air France to continue its commercial flights to Port-au-Prince after the United States, Panama and Canada withdrew their aircraft in conformity with the embargo. It was also unfair for the United States to insist on an exemption to the trade embargo for Haitian assembly industries while pressing other nations to respect it fully.
8. Embargos should never be lifted prematurely. Termination of an embargo should await the achievement of its objectives. Otherwise, such action can lead to embarrassments and disappointments and the need to renew it.

9.  The fact that an embargo is in place should not be used as an excuse for inaction or to buy time. "Let's wait for the sanctions to take effect" can conceal a desire to procrastinate or even not to act.
10. It is questionable whether comprehensive embargos or sanctions can achieve the desired results unless they are backed by a credible threat to use force.

## *Protection of Human Rights*

During the entire period of the Haitian crisis, the international community was concerned with protection of the rights of Haitian citizens. This concern focused on prevention of abuse of the rights of those residing in Haiti as well as the rights of those who sought refuge outside the country.

### Protection of Haitians in Haiti

From the day of Aristide's overthrow, and even after his return, the Haitian military and their assorted henchmen (*attachés*, auxiliaries, FRAPH, etc.) conducted a systematic reign of terror against Aristide sympathizers. Early on, after much negotiation, Dante Caputo was able to obtain agreement from Haitian interim Prime Minister Marc Bazin for 56 OAS/UN human rights observers to operate in the country. That force was eventually built up to 119. Nevertheless, human rights organizations reported that cruel beatings, torture and extra-judicial executions were common. At times *attachés* deliberately beat supporters of Aristide in front of human rights monitors to demonstrate that they could do so without fear of reprisal. UN/OAS observers were authorized to observe and report but not intervene.

After the Governors Island Agreement, violence intensified. Prominent pro-Aristide political figures and businessmen were targeted, and two were killed. Caputo linked Police Chief Francois to these and more than 100 murders that had taken place following the agreement. Private international rights organizations estimated 30 disappearances. Persons that reappeared reported interrogation under torture.

Opponents to Aristide's return were emboldened by having turned back the Harlan County. Haiti's new Minister of Justice, selected by Aristide as part of his new transition government, was gunned down along with his driver and one of his bodyguards. Finally, admitting the impossibility of maintaining order in Haiti, the United Nations withdrew most of its human rights monitors. Francois and his *attachés* were in control and there was nothing the United Nations could do to stem the terror. UN Secretary General Boutros Boutros-Ghali accused the Haitian military of waging an intensive campaign of repression against Aristide's followers, including at least a dozen cases of politically-motivated rape.

The most serious incident was the burning by members of FRAPH of over 200 homes of the poor in Cité Soleil, a slum inhabited principally by followers of Aristide. Four persons lost their lives, five were wounded and an estimated 5,000 were left homeless.

As the United States prepared to use force in Haiti, the Haitian military moved to increase its control over the civilian population and ordered the remaining UN human rights observers to leave the country. Subsequent to Boutros-Ghali's last report, these observers had reported 340 killings, 131 disappearances and 55 cases of politically-motivated rape.

## Protection of Haitian Refugees

Oppression by the military and abject poverty caused by the embargo resulted in thousands of Haitians fleeing their country and seeking refuge in the United States. One of the greatest challenges the United States faced was to distinguish between political and economic refugees. Under international law the United States was obligated to give political asylum to those with high probability of persecution if returned but was not obligated to accept those who fled for economic reasons.

Following is a brief chronological summary of the mass exodus of boat people from Haiti during the years 1991-1994 and how the United States sought to cope with the situation.

First, it is useful to point out that few people left Haiti during the first eight months that Aristide was in power in Haiti, and those few who did were economic rather than political refugees. As a matter of fact, many Haitians from the United States and Canada returned to Haiti during that brief period.

The military crackdown on Aristide supporters after the coup, combined with hardships caused by the embargo and the realization that the future held little hope for a quick return of their president, caused many followers of Aristide to take to the sea in boats in hope of reaching the United States. At first the number leaving was small, but as more and more were intercepted, the U.S. Coast Guard began to return them to their homeland. This practice was denounced by members of Congress, human rights organizations and the UN High Commissioner for Refugees. President Bush defended the practice as a way of saving Haitian lives. A federal judge in Miami ordered Bush to halt this policy of forced repatriation, so Bush ordered that henceforth Haitian refugees should be taken to Guantanamo Bay in Cuba. By the end of 1991, 7,891 Haitian refugees had been intercepted at sea and taken to the base.

When the OAS tightened its embargo on Haiti, the exodus increased sharply and the facilities at Guantanamo reached their capacity of 12,500. While his case was under appeal, Bush was allowed to continue the forced repatriations to Haiti. Human rights groups protested, but the number of boat people declined sharply. By August 1992, the only Haitian refugees remaining in Guantanamo were 233 with HIV or AIDs, including persons related to them.

As candidate for president, Bill Clinton sharply criticized Bush's policy of returning Haitian refugees to Haiti without a hearing, so that when he was elected the United States braced itself for a new wave of refugees. On November 17, President-elect Clinton said he would do nothing to increase the flow of refugees to the United States, but he was not believed in Haiti. U.S. intelligence sources estimated that 100,000 persons were ready to depart on boats for the United States. President Clinton found himself defending before U.S. courts the very policy of forced repatriation for which he had criticized Bush, and he won on appeal to the Supreme Court.

Nevertheless, the agitation against forced repatriation increased in the United States. Ninety-five prominent U.S. liberals sharply protested the policy in a near full-page advertisement in *The New York Times*. Aristide gave Clinton six months notice of his intention to abrogate a 1981 treaty giving U.S. officials the right to return illegal Haitian immigrants to Haiti. Two prominent U.S. human rights organizations also sharply criticized the policy. One of them, Amnesty International, reported that 139 of 904 Haitians in one group forcibly returned to Haiti had been arrested.

Six members of the U.S. House of Representatives were arrested by the U.S. Park Police while protesting U.S. policy toward Haiti in front of the White House, especially the President's policy of forced repatriation. A 27-day hunger strike by Randall Robinson, executive director of TransAfrica, was the principal factor in Clinton's reversal of the forced repatriation policy.

In mid-1994, under the guidance of William H. Gray, new U.S. point man on Haiti in the U.S. Department of State, steps were taken to multinationalize cooperation on the treatment of Haitian refugees. Mr. Gray announced an agreement with the UN High Commissioner for Refugees for cooperation in the processing of Haitian refugees and locating countries in which they could settle. On June 1 the governments of Jamaica and the United States announced a plan for shipboard processing of refugees in Jamaican ports, and on June 3 the government of the Turks and Caicos Islands agreed on a land-based processing center on Grand Turk Island.

## Lessons Learned

1. The use of human rights monitors by the international community to discourage human rights abuses by governments has limited value when the perpetrators of such abuses have no conscience. The government in power, if so motivated, is in a strong position to devise ways of wreaking vengeance on its citizens and avoiding detection. If the international community feels that such action should not be tolerated it will have to find some way of bringing such violators to justice.

2. Few persons seek to emigrate if economic and political conditions in their homeland are acceptable. Therefore, wealthy nations that fear the influx of refugees should aid poor countries in developing the kind of environment that will make their citizens want to stay at home. Foreign aid and humanitarian assistance can help. They are less expensive than maintaining flotillas on the high seas to intercept refugees and camps in which to house them. And the question of forced repatriation is eclipsed.

3. Race should not be a factor in granting refugees political asylum. The determining factor is whether brutality has occurred and whether that brutality is state sponsored.

4. Fleeing both oppression and the disastrous effects of an embargo, many Haitians were *both* political and economic refugees.

5. The U.S. Immigration Act of 1990 can serve as the legal framework for Temporary Protective Status without having to grant permanent political asylum.

6. If the international community should consider that force may be required to change conditions in a society with a cruel dictatorship such as the one in Haiti under Cédras and Francois, it may actually

be desirable to encourage migration of able-bodied young males from that nation in order to form a military force to liberate that country.

## The Use of Coercive Diplomacy

In his book, *Forceful Persuasion· Coercive Diplomacy as an Alternative to War*, published by the Institute of Peace Press, Washington, D.C., the distinguished political scientist Alexander George defines coercive diplomacy as "a defense strategy that involves threatening an opponent with dire consequences if he doesn't abandon an aggressive action." According to George, there are several types of coercive diplomacy, ranging in degree of pressure from a simple demand to a full-fledged ultimatum. It can be enhanced by the carrot and stick approach.

With respect to Haiti, from the very beginning of the 1991-1994 crisis, at the ad hoc Meeting of Foreign Ministers of the Organization of American States on October 2, 1991, two days after President Aristide was overthrown, U.S. Secretary of State James Baker set a bellicose tone for the future when he stated, "This coup will not succeed. This organization must not, and I am sure will not rest, until the people of Haiti regain their democracy." His words carried an implied threat of continued U.S. and OAS pressure until Aristide was restored. If initial steps did not succeed, Baker said, "the organization would consider additional steps."

For two years, the OAS and the United Nations relied on conventional diplomacy, embargos and sanctions to try to solve the Haitian crisis. After the rebuff of the Harlan County, however, virtually all U.S. action with respect to ending the crisis implied the possibility if not the probability of using military force. For example, shortly after the Harlan County incident, President Clinton sent six naval warships to Haiti and ordered an infantry company to Guantanamo Bay "to protect, if necessary, the lives of American personnel living in Haiti." Historically, protection of American lives had been used many times by the United States as rationale for military intervention.

By the beginning of 1994, it became evident that only military action, or the credible threat of military action, could dislodge the military dictators of Haiti from power. Prominent liberals in the U.S. Congress asked Clinton for more forceful leadership, including the use of U.S. troops. But, after the loss of 18 American lives in Somalia, Clinton was reluctant to become involved in Haiti. This was realized by the Haitian military leaders and to that extent Clinton's attempts to pursue coercive diplomacy lacked credibility.

Representative Joseph P. Kennedy of Massachusetts called for the threat of military intervention "to make the military recognize that the United States was willing to put its troops on the line." But Deputy Secretary of Defense Slocumbe stated that the United States had no desire to use military force in Haiti, in effect reassuring the military leadership in Haiti that they had nothing to fear.

In mid-1994, Clinton said for the first time that the military option was not ruled out with respect to Haiti. Various options were discussed but none were agreed upon. A divided Congress, divided public opinion and differing opinions within his own Administration made it difficult to take forceful action.

Finally, the Clinton administration engaged in some long-range planning. It asked U.S. allies to pledge troops for a future 3,000-member peacekeeping force to maintain order in Haiti after the military stepped down. Clinton did not discard the possibility of military action to force them to step down. On the contrary, he stressed that "the military option was still on the table." It was learned that the Department of Defense was giving that option serious study. All this was reported in the U.S. media and presumably known to Cédras and company.

Clinton decided on a show of strength. He sent a U.S. Marine Expeditionary Force of 1,900 soldiers aboard four ships to Haitian waters. The marines conducted mock evacuation exercises on a nearby island in the Bahamas, exactly the kind of operation that would be required to evacuate Americans from Haiti in case of invasion.

On July 31, 1994 the United Nations Security Council passed a long-awaited resolution to authorize the use of force in Haiti by its member states. Specifically, it approved a U.S. plan to raise a multinational force to "use all necessary means to facilitate the departure from Haiti of the military dictatorship." The resolution provided that the United Nations Mission in Haiti (UNMIH) would take over when a secure environment was established to protect international personnel and key installations, to professionalize the Haitian army and to establish a separate police force. The troop level of the UNMIH would be increased to 6,000.

President Aristide backed the resolution in a letter calling for prompt and decisive action. Madeleine Albright, U.S. Ambassador to the United Nations, said that the message to the top three military commanders was simple: "You can depart voluntarily and soon, or you can depart involuntary and soon." Argentina agreed to participate in the first phase with two warships, giving the force a multilateral dimension from the start. Pledges of participation were also secured from Barbados, Belize, Jamaica and Trinidad and later from Britain and four more Caribbean nations. Belgium, the Netherlands and France agreed to participate in the post-invasion phase.

All this diplomatic activity sent a message to Cédras that the international community was indeed serious about removing the three generals from power. U.S. Deputy Secretary of Defense John M. Deutch said, "There should be no question in anyone's mind that the multinational force is going to Haiti. . . . The only issues are the circumstances under which the force enters Haiti. It could go under permissive circumstances, or it could go under contested circumstances."

Twelve giant cargo ships were readied at U.S. ports to transport heavy equipment to the U.S. landing forces, which would number between 15,000 to 20,000 in the first stage. The aircraft carrier USS Eisenhower was sent to the Caribbean and the U.S. Army's 10th Mountain Division at Fort Drum, New York, was alerted. The USS Mount Whitney was ordered to Norfolk to be used as headquarters for the operation.

A "walk through" of planning for the invasion was conducted at Ft. McNair and 700 paratroopers from Ft. Bragg conducted practice jumps. All of this activity was given wide publicity in Haiti. U.S. Ambassador Swing at Port-au-Prince delivered separate ultimatums to the key military leaders Cédras, Biamby and Francois — to leave with U.S. assistance or face arrest. U.S. officials said U.S. forces would enter the country in a matter of days. Clinton made a television address to the nation on September 15, 1994 in which he told the "military thugs" to "leave now or we shall force you from power."

## Lesson Learned

Coercive diplomacy, if backed by military power, can be highly effective in achieving political and military objectives. But dissident voices can lower its credibility and cancel out its effectiveness.

## Use of Unofficial Envoys

On September 16, 1994, President Clinton announced that a negotiating team composed of former President Jimmy Carter, former chairman of the Joint Chiefs of Staff, General Colin Powell, and Senator Sam Nunn, chairman of the U.S. Senate Foreign Relations Committee, would go to Haiti to make a last-minute try to negotiate terms for the departure from office of Generals Cédras and Biamby and Police Chief Michel Francois. It was emphasized that the negotiations would not affect the time-table for the planned invasion. The purpose was to arrange, if possible, for permissive entry of U.S. troops into Haiti, to allow a smooth transition to U.S. control and avoid casualties on both sides. Cédras and Biamby (Francois did not participate in the negotiations but indicated he would accept the terms of any agreement made) were offered two choices: either to stay during the brief period between agreeing to resign and the arrival of U.S. forces, or not resign and face the possibility of personal harm to themselves and their families. During the negotiations Carter kept in close contact with President Clinton by telephone over a secure line.

Cédras capitulated when Biamby informed him that the invasion was underway. The negotiators secured the signature of provisional President Jonaissant on a draft agreement; Carter informed Clinton; and paratroopers of the 82d Airborne Division were ordered back to their bases just one hour before their scheduled landings in Haiti. (A more detailed account of the activities of the negotiating team appears in Chapter X and the text of the agreement in Appendix V.) The result was unopposed landings from helicopters at the international airport in Port-au-Prince by soldiers of the 10th Mountain Division the following morning. Lt. Gen. Henry H. Shelton, leader of the force, was met by Brig. Gen. Jean-Claude Duperval. Shelton drove to Haitian military headquarters and met with Cédras. During a two-hour meeting the two agreed to terms of cooperation during the period before he, Biamby and Francois submitted their resignations.

## Lessons Learned

1.  Unofficial envoys can be effective in resolving international conflicts if they are perceived as being distinguished, fair-minded and sensitive to the position of the adversary. Former President Carter had just negotiated an agreement to end the conflict between the United States and North Korea which was acceptable to both sides. Colin Powell was superior to Cédras in both rank and reputation and was essentially non-political. Nunn held a powerful position in the U.S. Senate and had no record of strong, anti-Cédras rhetoric.
2.  Unofficial envoys can be successful in avoiding bloody armed conflict when other means, including conventional diplomacy, embargoes, sanctions, even coercive diplomacy, fail.
3.  Unofficial envoys are more difficult to control than conventional envoys.
4.  If use of unofficial envoys is left literally to the eleventh hour, a last-minute change in basic mission can cause confusion among arriving troops. In this case the image of Cédras had changed overnight from "thug" to partner.
5.  Carter, Powell and Nunn were able to save countless American and Haitian lives through their non-official diplomacy.

## *Assertive Multilateralism*

This is a term coined by Madeleine Albright, U.S. Ambassador to the United Nations, to characterize the active participation of the United States in support of peacekeeping efforts by the United Nations and other international organizations. It anticipates a continuing leadership role by the United States in shaping the policy decisions of those organizations. The U.S. is to view the various international bodies dedicated to crisis prevention as user friendly. Increasing involvement by the United Nations and other organizations in peace keeping operations is considered in the U.S. national interest as helping to shape the international security environment.

The policy of assertive multilateralism was applied to the Haitian crisis throughout its duration and was manifested in particular in U.S. policies toward the United Nations and the Organization of American States. The United States played a leading role in the development of Haitian policy by these two organizations. U.S. Secretary of State James

Baker was instrumental in persuading the OAS to adopt an aggressive policy toward the Haitian military junta and he participated in the OAS Foreign Ministers mission to Haiti that sought to persuade the military leaders to permit the return of President Aristide to his legitimate post. From her position on the UN Security Council, Ambassador Albright initiated many of the resolutions condemning the actions of the Haitian military leadership, supporting OAS efforts, applying and expanding a trade embargo and sanctions on Haiti and above all, UN Security Council Resolution 940, which approved a U.S. plan for multinational intervention in Haiti and for peacekeeping operations following the restoration of law and order in the nation.

The United States hosted the meeting between President Aristide and General Cédras at Governors Island, which led to the agreement by that name. The United States also sought to assist in the training of the Haitian army and police under Section 5c of the agreement. Unfortunately it was not able to carry out that mission because the ship carrying the men and materials, the Harlan County, was prevented from landing at the dock in Port-au-Prince by members of the Haitian paramilitary organization FRAPH (see Chapter VI, Rebuff of the Harlan County).

U.S. Deputy State Strobe Talbott and U.S. Secretary of Defense John M. Deutch attended a meeting of the Caribbean Community in Kingston, Jamaica and secured pledges from four of its members (Barbados, Belize, Jamaica and Trinidad and Tobago) to contribute troops to the UN-sanctioned military intervention in Haiti. After conditions in Haiti were stabilized, the United States aided in the recruitment of international monitors to supervise training and subsequent duties of a new Haitian police force. The United States also developed cooperative relations with the UN High Commissioner on Refugees.

## Lessons Learned

1.  At times actions taken within the framework of international agreements and international organizations involving many nations can be more effective than actions taken unilaterally.
2.  Multilateralism serves an important function in getting other nations to share responsibility.
3.  Above all, multilateralism can help bestow legitimacy to international actions.

## *General Conclusions*

This book tells the story of a democratically-elected president of a small impoverished Caribbean nation who was deposed by a military coup and restored to his legitimate position by an international coalition led by the United States. Great! But the effort took *three* years, while many innocent lives were lost in the interim. Why did it take so long?

The decision to act to reverse the coup was taken within two days of the coup by the Organization of American States. The tools chosen to accomplish this objective were conventional democracy and the trade embargo. Neither was effective. In fact, the embargo was counterproductive. The poor suffered while the military prospered.

It took nearly three years for the international community to realize that it was using the wrong tools. A reading of Haitian history over the past 200 years shows that, until Jean-Bertrand Aristide was democratically elected on December 20, 1990, nearly all previous Haitian governments had come to power through the use of force and had maintained themselves in power by force until deposed by force. It was perhaps predictable that force would be used to depose Aristide. Indeed, one serious attempt was made to depose him by force even before he was inaugurated. Those who cherish democracy should have helped protect him both before and after he took office, until he was secure in that position. Certainly, after he was violently driven from the presidency, the international community should have taken immediate and decisive action to restore him as soon as possible.

As bureaucracies go, the Organization of American States moved rapidly to convene, first its Permanent Council, then its Council of Foreign Ministers, to consider the Haitian crisis. But it went no further in these early days than to send a mission to Haiti, freeze Haitian government assets in its member countries, and impose a trade embargo on the country, all laudable measures in themselves but, as events proved, inadequate to meet the objective of restoring Aristide to power.

The psychological moment to act to restore a democratically-elected ruler forcibly removed from his rightful position is to return him to that position as soon as possible. President Bush met with President Aristide at the White House on October 4, 1991 but did not offer military assistance to restore him.

Randall Robinson, executive director of TransAfrica wrote as follows in the Outlook section of *The Washington Post* of October 15, 1994:

Last week Michael Manley, the former prime minister of Jamaica, told me of a proposal that he, Canadian Prime Minister Brian Mulroney and Venezuela President Carlos Andres Perez made after Aristide was overthrown in September 1991.

They let it be known officially that they were willing to commit soldiers from each of their countries to an American-led military presence in Haiti for the purpose of restoring Aristide to power. Nothing ever came of their offer.

Robinson did not specify exactly when, to whom and through what medium the offer was made but if his report is correct, failure to follow up on this offer represents a missed opportunity of mammoth proportions. Thousands of lives might have been saved in Haiti and on the high seas if this proposal had been acted upon. Assertive multilateralism was lacking.

Two years passed before another opportunity of this magnitude arose. Ironically, it was presented to the international community by Cédras himself when he violated his commitment under step 5c of the Governors Island Agreement to accept "assistance for the modernizing of the Armed Forces of Haiti and establishing a new Police Force with the presence of United Nations personnel in these fields." With the approval of one of the two signatories, Aristide (the other being Cédras), and obtaining port clearance from authorities in Haiti, the United States sent to Port-au-Prince an unarmed contingent of 193 U.S. and 25 Canadian soldiers, all technical specialists. They arrived at the dock in October 13, 1993 aboard the U.S. transport Harlan County but were blocked from landing by about 100 armed persons on the wharf (See Chapter VI).

President Clinton ordered the Harlan County to withdraw. It was a mistake. He should have enforced his right to carry out the mission under international law. The Governors Island Agreement is a treaty. The United States was acting as the agent of one of the signatories of that treaty, and it had been violated by the other party. Adhering to the timetable of the Governors Island Agreement would have resolved the Haitian crisis one year earlier.

Another option available from the beginning and advocated by a number of persons, this author included, was recruitment and training of able-bodied volunteers from among Haitian refugees and exiles in Haitian communities in the United States, Canada and other countries. The object would have been to encourage liberation of Haiti by the Haitians themselves. The advantage of such a force is that its members would speak French and Creole, the languages of Haiti, would be for the most part familiar with Haiti, and would have been warmly welcomed and assisted by most of the population of Haiti, since the vast majority of the people were sympathetic to Aristide. U.S. military personnel could have provided training and broad logistical support to this force but would not have been part of it. This all-Haitian force could have been assembled at Guantanamo under the OAS/UN banner.

The most attractive feature of this idea was the probability that the force would never have to be used in combat. Faced with a formidable and credible threat of invasion from those of their own blood, and having weak and badly organized and equipped forces of their own, the Haitian military would probably have asked for a negotiated settlement.

What Haiti needs right now is a long period of peace and political stability during which democracy can become rooted, plus financial assistance to get the Haitian economy moving again.

# Appendices

## Appendix I
## Chapter VII, Charter of the United Nations

### Actions with Respect to Threats of Peace, Breaches of the Peace, and Acts of Aggression

*Article 39*

The Security Council shall determine the existence of any threat to the peace, breach of the peace, or act of aggression and shall make recommendations, or decide what measures shall be taken in accordance with Articles 41 and 42, to maintain or restore international peace and security.

*Article 40*

In order to prevent an aggravation of the situation, the Security Council may, before making the recommendations or deciding upon the measures provided for in Article 39, call upon the parties concerned to comply with such provisional measures as it deems necessary or desirable. Such provisional measures shall be without prejudice to the rights, claims, or position of the parties concerned. The Security Council shall duly take account of failure to comply with such provisional measures.

*Article 41*

The Security Council may decide what measures not involving the use of armed force are to be employed to give effect to its decisions, and it may call upon the Members of the United Nations to apply such measures. These may include complete or partial interruption of economic relations and of rail, sea, air, postal, telegraphic, radio, and other means of communication, and the severance of diplomatic relations.

*Article 42*

Should the Security Council consider that measures provided for in Article 41 would be inadequate or have proved to be inadequate, it may take such action by air, sea or land forces as may be necessary to maintain or restore international peace and security. Such action may include demonstrations, blockade, and other operations by air, sea, or land forces of Members of the United Nations.

## Article 43

1. All members of the United Nations, in order to contribute to the maintenance of peace and security, undertake to make available to the Security Council, on its call and in accordance with a special agreement or agreements, armed forces, assistance and facilities, including rights or passage, necessary for the purpose of maintaining international peace and security.
2. Such agreement or agreements shall govern the numbers and types of forces, their degree of readiness and general location, and the nature of the facilities and assistance to be provided.
3. The agreement or agreements shall be negotiated as soon as possible on the initiative of the Security Council. They shall be concluded between the Security Council and Members or between the Security Council and groups of Members and shall be subject to ratification by the signatory states in accordance with their respective constitutional processes.

## Article 44

When the Security Council has decided to use force it shall, before calling upon a Member not represented on it to provide armed forces in fulfillment of the obligations assumed under Article 43, invite that Member, if the Member so desires, to participate in the decisions of the Security Council concerning the employment of contingents of that Member's armed forces.

## Article 45

In order to enable the United Nations to take urgent military measures, Members shall hold immediately available national air-force contingents for combined international enforcement action. The strength and degree of readiness of these contingents and plans for their combined action shall be determined, within the limits laid down in the special agreement or agreements referred to in Article 43, by the Security Council with the assistance of the Military staff Committee.

## Article 46

Plans for the application of armed force shall be made by the Security Council with the assistance of the Military Staff Committee.

## Article 47

1.  There shall be established a Military Staff Committee to advise and assist the Security Council on all questions relating to the Security Council's military requirements for the maintenance of international peace and security, the employment and command of forces placed under its disposal, the regulation of armaments, and possible disarmament.
2.  The Military Staff Committee shall consist of the Chiefs of Staff of the permanent members of the Security Council or their representatives. Any member of the United Nations not permanently represented on the Committee shall be invited by the Committee to be associated with it when the efficient discharge of the Committee's responsibilities requires the participation of that member in its work.
3.  The Military Staff Committee shall be responsible under the Security Council for the strategic direction of any armed forces placed at the disposal of the Security Council. Questions relating to the command of such forces shall be worked out subsequently.
4.  The Military Staff Committee, with the authorization of the Security Council and after consultation with the appropriate regional agencies, may establish regional sub-committees.

## Article 48

1.  The action required to carry out the decisions of the Security Council for the maintenance of peace and security shall be taken by the Members of the United Nations or by some of them, as the Security Council may determine.
2.  Such decisions may be carried out by the Members of the United Nations directly and through their action in the appropriate international agencies of which they are members.

## Article 49

The Members of the United Nations shall join in affording mutual assistance in carrying out the measures decided upon by the Security Council.

## Article 50

If preventive or enforcement measures against any state are taken by the Security Council, any other state, whether a Member of the Security Council or not, which finds itself confronted with special economic problems arising from the carrying out of these measures shall have the right to consult the Security Council with regard to a solution of those problems.

## *Article 51*

Nothing in the present Charter shall impair the inherent right of individual or collective self-defense if an armed attack occurs against a Member of the United Nations, until the Security Council has taken measures necessary to maintain international peace and security. Measures taken by members in the exercise of this right of self-defense shall be immediately reported to the Security Council and shall not in any way affect the authority and responsibility of the Security Council under the present Charter to take at any time such actions as it deems necessary in order to maintain or restore international peace and security.

# *Appendix II*

## Articles of the Constitution of Haiti of 1987 Most Pertinent to the Presidency

### *Article 41*

No person of Haitian nationality may be forced to leave the national territory for any reason.

### *Article 134-1*

The term of the President is five (5) years. This term begins and ends on the February 7 following the date of the elections.

### *Article l34-2*

Presidential elections shall take place the last Sunday in November in the fifth year of the President's term.

### *Article 134-3*

The President of Haiti may not be reelected. He may serve an additional term only after an interval of five (5) years. He may in no case run for a third term.

### *Article 135-1*

Before taking office, the President of the Republic shall take the following oath before the National Assembly: "I swear before God and the nation faithfully to observe and enforce the Constitution and the laws of the Republic, to respect and cause to be respected the rights of the Haitian people, to work for the greatness of the country, and to maintain the nation's independence and the integrity of its territory.

### *Article 143*

The President of the Republic is the nominal head of the armed forces, but he never commands them in person.

### *Article 147*

He may grant amnesty only for political matters as stipulated by law.

### Article 149

Should the office of the President become vacant for any reason, the President of the Supreme Court of the Republic . . . shall be invested temporarily with the duties of the President of the Republic by the National Assembly duly convened by the Prime Minister.

### Article 149-1

The acting President may in no case be a candidate in the next presidential election.

### Article 150

The President of the Republic shall have no powers other than those accorded to him by the Constitution.

# *Appendix III*

## Excerpts from the Ten Commandments of Democracy Speech by President Jean-Bertrand Aristide before the General Assembly of the United Nations at New York, September 25, 1991

. . . At the moment when the international community is absorbed in the shifting of the geopolitical axis of the planet, let us turn to our dear Haiti, that rebellious and faithful daughter,

> *Rebellious toward every imperialist dictate,*
> *Faithful to every democratic precept.*

Let us also speak primarily of ten glowing beacons christened "the ten commandments of democracy," arising out of our democratic praxis. Indeed, our message is limited to the democratic arena where they stand in a straight line, these "ten growing beacons christened "the ten commandments of democracy."

### *The First Commandment of Democracy:*
### *Liberty or Death*
As you know, Haiti was one of the first beacons of liberty in the western hemisphere. In 1791, we presented to the world the first slave revolution, through which hundreds of thousands of blacks freed themselves from the yoke of oppression. The leaders of that victorious revolution helped to finance the liberating crusades of Simon Bolivar in South America. It was in Haiti that slavery was abolished for the first time, a giant step toward the liberation of humanity. The roots of the Declaration of Human Rights arose from Haitian revolution. The Haiti of Boukmann, of Dessalines, of Toussaint-Louverture is and remains the first black republic of the world. . . .

### *The Second Commandment of Democracy:*
### *Democracy or Death*
Finally, on December 16, 1990, thanks to the heroic courage of the Haitian people, thanks to their contribution, we for the first time carried out free, honest and democratic elections! Honor to the Haitian masses!

Glory to our ancestors, who put a stop to colonialism throughout the nineteenth century! Bravo to the international community! Bravo and applause to the United Nations!

Indeed, this was a great beginning in history. For once, through a brilliant tactical movement, a nation had carried out a revolution through the ballot box. The election of the first president of the republic by more than 70 percent on the first ballot symbolized simultaneously: *The victory of the people, The power of the people, The demands of the people. . . .*

### The Third Commandment of Democracy:
### Fidelity to Human Rights

If human beings have duties, they certainly have rights: rights to respect and to be respected. It is, in the last analysis, to guarantee those rights that a just government is established.

### The Fourth Commandment of Democracy:
### The Right to Eat and to Work

The participation of the private sector is essential for the creation of highly labor-intensive industries. While in the past illicit practices have enabled certain sectors to despoil the country at the expense of the majority of the population, our *Lavalas* government on the contrary is on the alert to see that the rights of all are respected. These include the right to invest according to the constitutional norms, and the right to work for human and economic growth. To you, our dear friends and foreign investors, Haiti desires, now and in the future, to extend the warmest and most cordial welcome.

### The Fifth Commandment of Democracy:
### The Right to Demand What Rightfully Belongs to Us

As Haitian women and men who are awake, we have one world: the world of justice. Justice for everyone: for Haitians, women and men, too often victims of social injustice at the international level! If we scan the horizons of this world of justice we wonder how long the impoverished will have to cry out with Democritus: "We seek the good and do not find it; we find evil without seeking it."

## *The Sixth Commandment of Democracy:*
## *Legitimate Defense of the Diaspora, or Tenth Department*

Driven out until 1991 by the blind brutality of the repressive machine or by the structures of exploitation erected in an anti-democratic system, our Haitian sisters and brothers have not always had the good fortune to find a promised land. Illegal because the brutes have not had the forethought to give their victims certificates of torture properly signed; illegal because they have not had to travel as boat people or without being provided with legal documents, they have nevertheless made great contributions to the economic prosperity of their patrons, preferring to do all the hardest work rather than to take charity.

What shall we say to our sisters and brothers who are imprisoned at Krome and elsewhere? In the name of democracy, is there no room for bending a little with regard to their files and transforming their pain into joy? With a view to encouraging the authorities concerned to take steps in the direction of that hoped-for joy, we, the government of Haiti, are continually battling against fraudulent practices and the obtaining of false visas on Haitian soil. At the same time, we condemn the flagrant violation of the rights of Haitians living in the Dominican Republic.

## *The Seventh Commandment of Democracy:*
## *No to Violence, Yes to* Lavalas

A political revolution without armed force in 1991: is it possible? Yes. Incredible, but true. The pedagogy of *Lavalas*, the tactical and strategic convergence of democratic forces, brandished the weapon of unity against that of violence. A stunning victory! An historic surprise!

Schooled by the poor, the pedagogy of active non-violence and unity triumphed over institutionalized violence. After 1804, the date of our first independence, 1991 opened the era of our second independence.

## *The Eighth Commandment of Democracy:*
## *Fidelity to the Human Being, the Highest Form of Wealth*

We, too, are ready to prove our fidelity to humanity, embracing everything that promotes its full development. Hence the harmonious ties already fashioned with CARICOM are located within the framework of Caribbean solidarity for the purpose of better promoting human well-being.

We are also working at the intersection of our south-south relations, between our neighbors in South America and ourselves. South-south relations are not the only important ones for Haiti. In fact, we share a political heritage with the United States, whose independence reminds us of the Haitian pioneers who, precisely for the sake of that independence, were beaten and killed. Like France, with which we also share a political heritage together with the United States, the other countries of North America, Europe, the Middle East, Africa and other parts of the globe are situated together with us within the network of interdependence that binds all the nations of the globe.

### The Ninth Commandment of Democracy: Fidelity to Our Culture

The politics of *lavalas* endeavors to validate our cultural identity. No truly deep change can be accomplished democratically without an articulation of the indigenous values that are closely linked with any genuine socio-cultural fabric.

Fidelity to our culture urges us to sharpen our critical sense in order to protect the health of our culture against certain plagues, such as the illicit traffic in narcotics. The Haitian government is resolved to recall that an effective struggle against the production of drugs is also conditional on the extension of stronger assistance to the Latin American countries.

As concerns the drug traffic itself, it is important to recall that it is generated and fed by the demands of the North. It is also necessary, at all costs, to eliminate the incentives to production coming from consumers in the industrialized countries. Concerted action involving governments North and South, aided by the United Nations, would permit us to conduct a more effective struggle against this plague of assorted drugs that is eating away at men and women.

### The Tenth Commandment of Democracy: everyone Around the Same Table

> *Yes, everyone around the democratic table*
> *Not a minority on the table*
> *Not a majority under the table*
> *But everyone around the same table*

That, I think, is the historical meeting place as we approach 1992. . . .

Sisters and brothers of Jamaica, Barbados, Trinidad, Cuba, the Dominican Republic, Guadeloupe, Martinique: our past struggle against colonialism has led us inevitably toward the establishment of deeper ties in the course of our long march toward the democratic table.

A new social contract at the Caribbean, Latin American and international level is clearly necessary for us to join together one day, all of us, around the democratic table.

We others in Haiti, since December 16, 1990, the date of our elections under the supervision of the United Nations, are on the march toward that meeting place.

Mr. President,

I want to hope that the Fourth Decade of Development will produce concrete results in the realm of the new international order that is to be inaugurated.

Here at the end of the twentieth century, the Republic of Haiti renounces absolutism, embraces participatory democracy, and intones the hymn of liberty, pride and dignity.

## Appendix IV

## United Nations Security Council Resolution 940 Adopted by the Security Council at its 3413 meeting on July 31, 1994

*The Security Council,*

*Reaffirming* its resolutions 841 (1993 of 16 June 1993, 861 (1993) of 27 August 1993, 862 (1993) of 31 August 1993, 867 (1993) of 23 September 1993, 873 (1993) of 13 October 1993, 875 (1993) of 16 October 1993, 905 (1994) of 23 March 1994, 917 (1994) of 6 May 1994 and 933 (1994) of 30 June 1994,

*Recalling* the terms of the Governors Island Agreement (S/26297),

*Condemning* the continuing disregard of these agreements by the illegal de facto regime, and the regime's refusal to cooperate with efforts by the United Nations and the Organization of American States (OAS) to bring about their implementation,

*Gravely concerned* by the significant further deterioration of the humanitarian situation in Haiti, in particular the continuing escalation by the illegal de facto regime of systematic violations of civil liberties, the desperate plight of Haitian refugees and the recent expulsion of the staff of the International Civilian Mission (MICIVIH), which was condemned in its Presidential statement of 12 July 1994 (S/PRST/1994/32),

*Having considered* the reports of the Secretary-General of 15 July 1994 (S/1994/828 and Add.1) and 26 July 1994 (S/1994/871),

*Taking note* of the letter dated 29 July 1994 from the legitimately elected President of Haiti (S/1994/905, annex) and the letter dated 30 July 1994 from the Permanent Representative of Haiti to the United Nations (S/1994/910),

*Reiterating* its commitment for the international community to assist and support the economic, social and institutional development of Haiti,

*Reaffirming* that the goal of the international community remains the restoration of democracy in Haiti and the prompt return of the legitimately elected President, Jean-Bertrand Aristide, within the framework of the Governors Island Agreement,

*Recalling* that in resolution 873 (1993) the Council confirmed its readiness to consider the imposition of additional measures if the military authorities in Haiti continued to impede the activities of the United

Nations Mission in Haiti (UNMIH) or failed to comply in full with its relevant resolutions and the provisions of the Governors Island Agreement,

*Determining* that the situation in Haiti continues to constitute a threat to the peace and security of the region,

1.  *Welcomes* the report of the Secretary-General of 15 July 1994 (S/ 1994/828) and *takes note* of his support for action under Chapter VII of the Charter of the United Nations in order to assist the legitimate Government of Haiti in the maintenance of public order;
2.  *Recognizes* the unique character of the present situation in Haiti and its deteriorating, complex and extraordinary nature, requiring an exceptional response;
3.  *Determines* that the illegal de facto regime in Haiti has failed to comply with the Governors Island Agreement and is in breach of its obligations under the relevant resolutions of the Security Council;
4.  *Acting* under Chapter VII of the Charter of the United Nations, authorizes Member States to form a multilateral force under unified command and control and, in this framework, to use all necessary means to facilitate the departure from Haiti of the military leadership, consistent with the Governors Island Agreement, the prompt return of the legitimately elected President and the restoration of the legitimate authorities of the Government of Haiti, and to establish and maintain a secure and stable environment that will permit implementation of the Governors Island Agreement, on the understanding that the cost of implementing this temporary operation will be borne by the participating Member States;
5.  *Approves* the establishment, upon adoption of this resolution of an advance team of UNMIH of not more than sixty personnel, including a group of observers, to establish the appropriate means of coordination with the multinational force, to carry out the monitoring of the operations of the multinational force and other functions described in paragraph 23 of the report of Secretary-General of 15 July 1994 (S/1994/828), and to assess requirements and to prepare for the deployment of UNMIH upon completion of the mission of the multinational force;
6.  *Requests* the Secretary-General to report on the activities of the team within thirty days of the date of deployment of the multinational force;

7.  *Decides* that the tasks of the advance team as defined in paragraph 5 above will expire on the date of termination of the mission of the multinational force;

8.  *Decides* that the multinational force will terminate its mission and UNMIH will assume the full range of its functions described in paragraph 9 below when a secure and stable environment has been established and UNMIH has adequate force capability and structure to assume the full range of its functions; the determination will be made by the Security Council, taking into account recommendations from the Member States of the multinational force, which are based on the assessment of the commander of the multinational force, and from the Secretary-General;

9.  *Decides* to revise and extend the mandate of the United Nations Mission in Haiti (UNMIH) for a period of six months to assist the democratic Government of Haiti in fulfilling its responsibilities in connection with:

    (a) securing the secure and stable environment established during the multinational phase and protecting international personnel and key installations; and

    (b) the professionalization of the Haitian armed forces and the creation of a separate police force;

10. *Requests also* that UNMIH assist the legitimate constitutional authorities in Haiti in establishing an environment conducive to the organization of free and fair legislative elections to be called by those authorities and, when requested by them, monitored by the United Nations in cooperation with the Organization of American States (OAS);

11. *Decides* to increase the troop level of UNMIH to 6,000 and establishes the objective of completing UNMIH's mission, in cooperation with the constitutional Government of Haiti, no later than February 1996;

12. *Invites* all States, in particular those in the region, to provide appropriate support for the actions undertaken by the United Nations and by Member States pursuant to this and other relevant Security Council resolutions.

13. *Requests* the Member States acting in accordance with paragraph 4 above to report to the Council at regular intervals, the first such report to be made not later than seven days following the deployment of the multinational force;

14. *Requests* the Secretary-General to report on the implementation of this resolution at sixty-day intervals, starting from the date of deployment of the multinational force;
15. *Demands* strict respect for the persons and premises of the United Nations, the Organization of American States, other international and humanitarian organizations and diplomatic missions in Haiti, and that no acts of intimidation or violence be directed against personnel engaged in humanitarian or peacekeeping work;
16. *Emphasizes* the necessity that, *inter alia*:
    (a) All appropriate steps be taken to ensure the security and safety of the operations and personnel engaged in such operations; and
    (b) The security and safety arrangements undertaken extend to all persons engaged in the operations;
17. *Affirms* that the Council will review the measures imposed pursuant to resolutions 841 (1993), 873 (1993) and 917 (1994), with a view to lifting them in their entirety, immediately following the return to Haiti of President Jean-Bertrand Aristide.
18. *Decides* to remain actively seized of the matter.

# *Appendix V*

## The Carter Agreement: An Agreement Reached in
## Port-au-Prince, Haiti, September 18, 1994

1.  The purpose of this agreement is to foster peace in Haiti, to avoid violence and bloodshed, to promote freedom and democracy, and to forge a sustained and mutually beneficial relationship between the governments, people, and institutions of Haiti and the United States.

2.  To implement this agreement, the Haitian military and police forces will work in close cooperation with the U.S. military mission. This cooperation, conducted with mutual respect, will last during the transitional period required for insuring vital institutions of the country.

3.  In order to personally contribute to the success of this agreement, certain military officers of the Haitian armed forces are willing to consent to an early and honorable retirement in accordance with UN Resolutions 917 and 940 when a general amnesty will be voted into law by the Haitian Parliament, or October 15, 1994, whichever is earlier. The parties to this agreement pledge to work with the Haitian Parliament to expedite this action. Their successors will be named according to the Haitian Constitution and existing military law.

4.  The military activities of the U.S. Military Mission will be coordinated with the Haitian military high command.

5.  The economic embargo and the economic sanctions will be lifted without delay in accordance with relevant UN Resolutions and the need of the Haitian people will be met as quickly as possible.

6.  The forthcoming legislative elections will be in a free and democratic manner.

7.  It is understood that the above agreement is conditioned on the approval of the civilian governments of the United States and Haiti.

# Chronology

## Haitian Crisis, 1991-1995

*February 7, 1991*
Jean-Bertrand Aristide is inaugurated as president of Haiti.

*June 5, 1991*
The General Assembly of the Organization of American States passes Resolution 1080 instructing its Secretary General to take immediate action "in the event of any occurrence giving rise to the sudden or irregular interruption . . . of the legitimate exercise of power by the democratically-elected government of any of the organization's member states."

*September 25, 1991*
President Aristide addresses the United Nations General Assembly in New York and reports that democracy is fully rooted in Haiti.

*September 30, 1991*
The Haitian army forcibly removes President Aristide from power. He flees to Venezuela.

*October 2, 1991*
An emergency meeting of the Foreign Ministers of the Organization of American States in Washington, D.C. decides to send a mission to Haiti comprised of high-ranking officials from eight OAS countries to warn Haiti's military junta that it faces economic and political isolation if it does not agree to President Aristide's prompt return to Haiti.

*October 4, 1991*
President Bush receives President Aristide at the White House.

*October 6, 1991*
The OAS mission to Haiti reports that Haiti's military commanders refuse to surrender power.

*October 8, 1991*
Supreme Court Justice Joseph Nerette is sworn as provisional president of Haiti, but the real power remains in the hands of the military.

*February 3. 1992*

The Washington Agreement is signed by President Aristide and provisional Haitian prime minister René Theodore setting out conditions for the return of Aristide to Haiti.

*March 27, 1992*

The Haitian Supreme Court decides that the Washington Agreement is unconstitutional.

*May 4, 1992*

President Bush orders direct repatriation of Haitian refugees headed for the United States.

*July 3, 1993*

The Governors Island Agreement is signed by Haitian President Jean-Bertrand Aristide and Haitian armed forces commander Raoul Cédras providing for President Aristide's return to power on October 30, 1993.

*July 16, 1993*

The United Nations Security Council votes unanimously to impose a world-wide oil and arms embargo on Haiti, along with a global freeze of Haitian government assets. The embargo took effect on July 23.

*August 27, 1993*

As a result of progress made in implementing the Governors Island Agreement, the United Nations Security Council suspends its embargo on Haiti.

*September 13, 1993*

Antoine Izmery, a close friend of Aristide, is assassinated in Haiti.

*October 11, 1993*

The USS Harlan County, a 560-foot flat-bottomed cargo ship with no combat capability, is prevented by armed thugs from landing 193 U.S. and 25 Canadian unarmed troops sent to help train the Haitian police and army and help rebuild the country's infrastructure as called for by Step 5c of the Governors Island Agreement.

## *October 13, 1993*

The United Nations reimposes its embargo on Haiti.

## *October 14, 1993*

Guy Malary, Haiti's highly respected Minister of Justice, is killed by assassins linked to the Haitian military in broad daylight on a street in Port-au-Prince.

## *January 14-16, 1994*

President Aristide holds a conference of his supporters in Miami, Florida to form a broad coalition of pro-democracy supporters in Haiti and abroad.

## *March 23, 1994*

A nearly full-page advertisement addressed to President Clinton and signed by 95 prominent U.S. liberals appears in *The New York Times* denouncing his policies on Haiti.

## *April 12-May 9, 1994*

Randall Robinson, Executive Director of TransAfrica holds a 27-day hunger strike protesting U.S. policies toward Haiti.

## *April 29, 1994*

Ambassador Lawrence Pezzullo is dismissed from his position as U.S. envoy to Haiti. He is replaced by former U.S. Congressman William Gray III on May 8. 1994.

## *May 11, 1994*

Judge Emil Jonaissant, head of the Haitian Supreme Court is installed as provisional president of Haiti, replacing Supreme Court Justice Nerette.

## *May 21, 1994*

The United Nations levies a comprehensive embargo on Haiti barring the entry of all goods except food, medicine and cooking oil.

## *June 25, 1994*

To place additional pressure on Haiti's military leaders, the United States terminates all commercial flights to Haiti and fund transfers between the United States and Haiti.

## July 31, 1994

The United Nations Security Council passes a resolution (S/Res/ 940) approving a U.S. plan to raise a multilateral force to "use all necessary means to facilitate the departure from Haiti of the military dictatorship."

## August 28, 1994

The Reverend Jean-Marie Vincent, a prominent Catholic priest and supporter of Aristide, is shot and killed, presumably by military gunmen.

## September 15, 1994

President Clinton, in a televised speech to the nation, explains the reasons for a planned U.S. intervention in Haiti.

## September 16, 1994

President Clinton announces that a negotiating team composed of former President Jimmy Carter, former chairman of the U.S. Joint Chiefs of Staff, General Colin Powell, and U.S. Senator Sam Nunn would be going to Haiti to seek a last-minute departure of Haiti's military leaders.

## September 18, 1994

At 9:30 p.m. President Clinton announces that Generals Cédras and Biamby and Police Chief Michel Francois have agreed to leave their posts on October 15, that U.S. troops would land in Haiti the next morning and that Haiti's military leaders had pledged to cooperate with them.

## September 19, 1994

At 9:30 a.m., U.S. forces land unopposed at the International Airport of Port-au-Prince.

## October 4. 1994

Haitian Police Chief Michel Francois leaves Haiti to take up residence in the Dominican Republic.

## October 7, 1994

The Haitian parliament authorizes a political amnesty to Haiti's military leaders.

## *October 8, 1994*

General Biamby tenders his resignation from the Haitian army and it is accepted by General Cédras the following day.

## *October 10, 1994*

General Cédras resigns from the Haitian army and asks his followers to cooperate with U.S. military forces.

## *October 13, 1994*

Cédras and Biamby leave Haiti for Panama, and provisional president Jonaissant announces his resignation.

## *October 15, 1994*

President Aristide returns to Haiti to a tumultuous welcome.

## *October 16, 1994*

The United Nations lifts all sanctions from Haiti.

# Recent Bibliography

Aristide, Jean-Bertrand. *In the Parish of the Poor: Writings from Haiti*, Orbis Books, Maryknoll, New York, 1990.

Aristide, Jean-Bertrand. *Jean-Bertrand Aristide: An Autobiography*. Orbis Books, Maryknoll, New York, 1993. Translation from *Tout Homme Est Un Homme*, Editions du Seuil, Paris, 1992.

Coalition for Civilian Observers in Haiti. *Internal Exile in Haiti: A Country Held Hostage by its Own Army*. Washington Office in Haiti, Washington, D.C. 1992.

George, Alexander. *Forceful Persuasion: Coercive Diplomacy as an Alternative to War*. Institute of Peace Press, Washington, D.C. 1992.

Greene, Anne. *The Catholic Church in Haiti: Political and Social Change*. Michigan State University Press, East Lansing, Michigan, 1993.

Laguerre, Michel S. *The Military and Society in Haiti*. The University of Tennessee Press, Knoxville, 1993.

National Defense University, Institute for National Strategic Studies. *Peacekeeping:The Way Ahead?* McNair Paper, Washington, D.C. November, 1993.

Organization of American States. *Report on the Situation of Human Rights in Haiti*. Washington, D.C. 1990.

Plummer, Brenda Gayle. *Haiti and the United States: The Psychological Moment*. University of Georgia Press, Athens, Georgia, 1992.

# Index

# About the Author

Roland I. Perusse is Director of the Inter American Institute, a non-profit foundation specializing in Inter-American affairs, located in Washington, D.C. He holds a PhD from American University in Washington, D.C. and has had a career in the U.S. Foreign Service, as well as academia. He has taught at the University of Texas at El Paso and Inter American University of Puerto Rico, where he specialized on Caribbean affairs. He has visited Haiti professionally on the average of once a year for the past 25 years. He is widely published on Caribbean affairs, including an *Historical Dictionary on Haiti*.